Also by Albert Paul Messina

The Nonprofit Leader as Liberal Thinker:
Politics, Ethics and Strategy Reconsidered

Albert Paul Messina

The Decline and Fall of Charity

PH

Philanthropy House Press

Printed in the United States of America

ISBN: 978-0-9835075-2-9

To Robert T. Kiernan,
my friend and mentor,
this book is affectionately dedicated

Contents

Prologue
The Decline

I do not know the truth; only my memories.
~ John Williams

We fight for lost causes because we know that our defeat and dismay may be the preface to our successor's victory.
~ T.S. Elliot

Despite the view that letters are a lost art, this story is told in the form of letters to an old friend and mentor who is fading not into a mist of memory but into one of certain oblivion. My model is the Roman philosopher Seneca, whose letters about courage and justice and self-control sought an understanding, a Stoic wisdom for himself and for the person to whom his letters were addressed, his friend Lucilius. The letters that comprise this story are an attempt to return some wisdom and solace to my friend and mentor of more than thirty years, Patrick McSweeney, who taught me that convictions count and loyal opposition, even when it cannot possibly prevail, is a noble stance to take. For my part I have decided, as the author of these letters and therefore the narrator of the story, to take on the same persona I established in my last book, *The Nonprofit Leader as Liberal Thinker*, that of the nonprofit executive, Michael Palermo.

Many of the letters appear as they were originally written, others with minor revision. Still others have been reconstructed from notes and speeches and position papers to fill out the narrative of a decline and fall, the decline of the idea of charity and of its institutional form, the nonprofit agency, and the fall of a friend and mentor to one of modernity's plagues, Alzheimer's disease. Other liberties taken in support of the narrative include a slightly rearranged chronology and the recognition that any story relying on one's memory, and thus one's imagination, is at best an imaginative reconstruction rather than a contemporaneous recording of what actually happened.

There is also the ongoing commentary, gleaned from Patrick's papers and borrowed from his barroom tutorials and from the many occasions on which he gave me good counsel, that is interspersed with my letters to him, as are many maxims and sub-headings, short essays and personal reflections, thus combining into one narrative a classic commonplace book of correlated ideas, an extended essay on the decline of a once democratic institution to which I dedicated my entire professional life, and a memoir of a man whose intellect and humanity I came to admire, Patrick "Paddy" McSweeney.

If, as Shakespeare observed, past is prologue, then the idea for *The Decline and Fall of Charity* really began thirty-five years ago with this comment from a nonprofit colleague: "We're no longer just a social service organization. We're a business." That casual observation, made to me just a few months into the start of my nonprofit career, was more prophetic than descriptive, because in early twenty-first century America the once venerable idea of a nonprofit institution has devolved into a corporate entity wholly preoccupied with money, marketing, and metrics. This ongoing devolution, consistent with the corporatization of other centers of American life from publishing to higher education and more recently to public education, has led to the decline of democratic norms and to the rise of junk science in all of these institutions. In their own realm, corporations create wealth, generate jobs and contribute to charitable institutions, but their insinuation into other realms of American life has had consequences that are largely negative.

The unpleasant truth is that the nonprofit

world is no longer what it once was and nothing like what it was even a few decades ago. It is no longer driven essentially by volunteerism, democratic norms, and the desire to ameliorate the conditions of the most vulnerable in our society. It is instead driven by physical, spiritual, artistic and educational aspirations, sending most of its resources to churches, hospitals, and colleges and universities.

The very idea of charity, apart from the nonprofit institutions that have so proliferated in the presumption of delivering it, has fallen even further. Whereas charity was once an informal act of kindness, it has now become a professionalized act of philanthropy. Whereas it was once given without expectation of anything tangible in return, it is now given with the expectation of much in return: the new entitlement of ever expanding public recognition of donors, the ever expanding demand for quantifiable results that lack any scientific legitimacy whatsoever, and finally, the ultimate expectation, the craven desire for the tenuous immortality that comes with having one's name affixed to some architectural marvel.

All this points to the need for a redefinition of charity as a disinterested, perhaps even noble act, and to the need for an institutional redefinition based on the needs of clients rather than the desires and aspirations of institutions.

And for those of us who have worked on behalf of children, it is a clarion call to end the idea of regarding children as cognitive data points, as institutional outcomes, as means to organizational ends. It is a call to see them in their full humanity, as ends in themselves, as works of art in the making.

To achieve such a redefinition of charity and of its delivery system, the nonprofit, would take a transformation or, if you like, a paradigm shift capable of contending with the movements that have defined modernity: the Enlightenment, the Scientific Revolution, and the rise of capitalism, all of which bequeathed to us in their own way a Darwinian world of winners and losers (too many losers) and an idea that "numbers," as Descartes aptly observed, "are the only test of certainty."

This, of course, is the classic lost cause. It is a war that would have to be won on at least two major fronts, the political and the intellectual. It would require getting the political class to stand down and allow public education to open up to real educational innovation rather than supporting its privatization by corporate philistines. It would take the intellectual class having the courage to reinvigorate higher education's dedication to the liberal arts, thus giving teachers, social workers, and nonprofit executives the intellectual resources to fight the good fight against the idea that the corporation ought to be the template for all of our educational and human service institutions.

The front established in this story is on the nonprofit field, on the field occupied by one of America's premier youth development agencies, which I will again call, as I did in *The Nonprofit Leader,* The Youth Association International, or simply The Association, or, as you will see frequently in the letters, by the more playful, ironic name of Whitehall.

The principal players and entities in this story of corporate intentions gone awry and of a deepening democratic decline include the periodic encounters (I hesitate to call them meetings) of the Cornell Crew, a group of fifteen local Association executives who originally gathered at Cornell for an executive leadership program and who became, through the will and intellect and quiet charisma of Patrick McSweeney, a self-directed think tank for more than two decades.

Other prominent entities in the story include the many commissions commissioned by Whitehall that not only diminished the legitimate governing entity of the local affiliates of the federation, the International Council, but ultimately rewrote the constitution that created the Council. It was a rewriting that concentrated power rather than diffused it. It was a rewriting that deconstructed an imperfect but well-intentioned democratic document into nothing more than a tool of corporate compliance.

And with that bit of background, let me turn now to the fight, to the front itself, and to the original leader of the loyal opposition, to one Patrick Michael McSweeney.

1

Social Institutions and the Decline of Democratic Governance

If citizens do not exercise the powers conferred by their legitimacy, others will do so.
~John Ralston Saul

Trashing A Constitution

...from a democratically constituted federation to a vertically integrated corporation.

Patrick, this year's annual conference was not the same without at least one of your late night barroom tutorials. Your retirement has left a void among those of us inclined to support a loyal opposition to Whitehall's increasing corporatization. I use the phrase "those of us" loosely, since I am beginning to believe that without you I am a loyal opposition of one.

The single most important event of this year's conference took place at a general session celebrating the centennial of the international organization. Steve Davis, the chairman of the international board, was introduced at the opening of this session, but he was not there for preliminary purposes, nor was he there to offer a perfunctory welcome to the troops. He was there instead to change our governing constitution without any discussion or debate.

Davis, you will recall, is a charismatic corporate CEO, a tall, handsome, articulate spokesman who disarmingly commanded the attention of the delegates as he stood center stage instead of behind the podium that was used by every other person in the program. From my vantage point, he's the Madison Avenue antithesis of Willy Loman with shinier shoes and an even whiter smile crowned and capped. He's the quintessential successful CEO with a commanding presence that says, "I want what I want when I want it." The overall impression one gets of him is that if self-regard were a work of art, Davis would be a DaVinci.

So, after effortlessly winning over the crowd, Davis called the meeting of the International Council to order. He quickly read a motion calling for the use of the Standards of Organizational Effectiveness as a constitutional requirement for membership in The Association. Just as quickly someone shouted out "second" from one of the rows near the stage and Davis simply said, "All those in favor say aye," at which point the crowd, rather than saying aye, roared, and in its celebratory frenzy added a fifty- page footnote to our constitution.

As I sat there and watched the celebratory trashing of our organization's founding document, I was reminded of the first International Council Meeting that I attended in Chicago in 1978. It was nothing like what I had just witnessed. I remember you getting up at one point to speak, to raise some objection. There were, as I recall, about 600 people in the ballroom, most of them credentialed delegates representing local Association organizations. I sat in the roped-off gallery watching a wonderful exercise in democracy as local executives such as yourself cordially parried and debated with members of the international board. After discussion and debate that lasted an entire morning, votes were taken, decisions made, a democratic norm reaffirmed.

Now we have no credentials, no delegates, no Council in any real sense. This is what happens when the corporation becomes the template for all of our institutions, including nonprofit federations such as ours. Whereas we were once a democratically-constituted federation, we have now become a vertically integrated corporation that drives change by a carefully orchestrating one commission process after another. This latest commission process launched by Whitehall was the second such attempt in three years. It was supposedly a response to local scandals, but was really, as the latest constitutional changes reveal, nothing more than a naked attempt to increase the number of standards for purposes of corporate control.

I promise to tell you more next time about the farcical way in which this latest commission has been conducted by Whitehall, but you'll also notice that I referred to constitutional *changes*. It seems that they did more than just add the Standards to the constitution. They added something else that, as far as I can tell, was never voted on at any International Council Meeting, even at one of Steve Davis's two-minute charm school performances.

Peace & Overthrow,
Michael

Constitution As Compliance Document

Nine words became ten, one clause became two, and the whole meaning of what was in the purview of the constitution changed.

Patrick, I just got back from our state Association meeting in Harrisburg, a meeting that the International Association's facilitator characterized as a town hall meeting. It was not in any real sense a town hall meeting but rather a highly scripted focus group in which we were asked a series of set questions. In fact, we were not permitted to ask a question until all of Whitehall's questions were posed and answered. I, of course, tried but was told to wait until the end of the meeting. The questions came from a paper sent out to us in advance called the "Constitutional Commission Briefing Paper. "The questions themselves make it pretty transparent as to where we're heading and have been heading for a long time.

The first question was: As a Movement, where are we vulnerable? This, for me, is the ethics question that our good friend Eileen Boyer (Do you realize that Eileen has been the International president now for fifteen years, the longest presidential tenure in the history of our organization?) has been driving since the big scandal surrounding the New York City Association. Every speech I've written for her in the last couple of years has trumpeted this theme of public trust. Here she is in her last speech, her idea, my words: "Our most prized possession is our integrity and the name Youth Association International, which is emblematic of that integrity. What we must never forget, what must remain indelible in our memory, is that our reputation took a century to build but could be undone in a day."

The next question starts to lay out the tactic

to be used to protect the so-called public trust in our reputation: What do we need to do to assure greater accountability of our member organizations?

The answer to greater accountability? That's contained in question number three: How do we standardize procedures and practices on the local level?

Then how do we standardize? We simply ask: Which requirements or standards need to be strengthened? Many, I would think. And then this: Are any new ones needed? Why of course. New is always good, is it not? Let's demand some new standards. Standards are good. Who could reasonably be against standards?

The next question moved from tactics to strategy: What does autonomy mean today? That reveals a new strategic outlook to the relationship between local organizations like ours and the International organization. The very construction of this question, qualified by the adverb today, along with the prior references to our vulnerability to scandal and the need for more standards, suggests that autonomy is out and accountability in.

After these profundities were posed and discussed by the fifty or so of us in the room, we were allowed roughly five minutes of actual town hall meeting time. This gave me the opportunity to note that governance by focus group is demeaning and undemocratic, that the whole question of operating standards is not even a constitutional question, and finally, that if this were indeed a constitutional commission, it ought to have representation from the field other than the International Council Committee that Whitehall formed a few years ago without anyone realizing it. Our facilitator, a board volunteer from one of the Pennsylvania Associations and a member of Whitehall's International Council Committee, got the last word, which was not, as one would imagine, salutary. "The challenge that the International organization has," he said, "is how to control thousands of local organizations so they're consistent."

That pretty much says it, Paddy. If we're not already there, we will soon arrive at that standardized, bureaucratized and sanitized destination of a single, unified corporation under the command and control of International Headquarters in New York. The whole question of standards is so problematic on so many levels that I really don't know where to begin. Just a cursory review of older versions of our constitution reveals that the idea of "operating" standards is something newly created. In the context of earlier versions of our constitution, the idea of standards is encapsulated in a single clause: "establish requirements and standards for membership in the corporation." Requirements and standards, by the construction of the clause, are being used synonymously—a requirement of membership, a standard of membership: it is one idea, not two, as in the current version of our constitution. In earlier versions of the constitution there is no mention of the word "operating." In the current version, one clause became two: "establish requirements for membership; establish operating standards." Nine words became ten, one clause became two, and the whole meaning of what was in the purview of the constitution changed. In fact, the whole meaning of the constitution itself changed. It is now not a constitution at all but rather a corporate compliance document.

I guess we missed the International Council Meeting where this rather subtle but profound change was voted into our constitution, though that seems unlikely, since between us we've been to every council meeting in the last forty-five years. Perhaps it was the well-intentioned work of some overly industrious copy editor. For if there is anything our international organization does not have a dearth of, it's industriousness, especially in the analytical realm of standards. I think it could be said that they never met a standard they didn't like. There are roughly two hundred and fifty standards in the Standards of Organizational Effectiveness, depending on how you count them, which now stands as a constitutional oddity: a fifty-page amendment, in the form of a footnote, to our constitution. Whatever the merits of the Standards—and they do have some limited merit as a reference tool—they have no sensible or rightful place in a constitution. Classical antiquity's greatest constitutional thinker, Aristotle, understood a constitution to be a general framework, not a prescriptive document consisting of particular rules and standards. Even that original Robber Barron, Alexander Hamilton, thought that constitutions should only consist of general provisions.

One thing I forgot to mention. The very last paragraph of the Constitutional Commission Briefing Paper noted that the International Council Committee, which Whitehall with its benign but apparently unlimited authority has also designated as the Constitutional Commission, will be meeting in November to review the results of the so-called town hall meetings. I'm going to try to finagle my way onto the Commission, even if I have to ask Eileen Boyer to appoint me. Let's forget about the Peace for now and just go with the Overthrow.

Michael

Michael, you obviously have some issues to contend with. Getting on the Commission? That you can probably manage as long as Eileen doesn't fully know where you're coming from going into it.

The operating standards stuff? Perhaps a little too esoteric. Maybe there are broader tacks to take. This is really an issue pitting the old democratic idea of autonomy against the corporate tide of headquarters control. Your biggest problem is that your memory of that organizational exercise in democracy, the 1978 Council Meeting, is not shared by most of the executives in the field today. We've had so much growth over the last two decades and so many new people in the field that there is no institutional memory of how we used to do things.

Analytic Overkill

This book is one whole thing, not just a lot of parts.
~ Ernest Hemingway

You may be right, as you almost always are, about the esoteric nature of the meaning of a single word in our constitution. This subtle, but I would argue profound change in our constitution from standards of membership to operating standards, will probably have no resonance with our brethren in the field. But I'm still troubled by the bureaucratic sleight-of-hand that allowed such a thing to happen, and I'm troubled even more about Whitehall's rather cavalier attitude toward our constitution and the democratic process it once guaranteed but has since allowed to languish and disappear.

Theoretically, we, the local organizations,

the field, if you will, govern The Youth Association International Movement. In practice, the international organization now does all the governing, and they do it in a way that disregards the traditional procedural rules that once characterized the democratic deliberations of the International Council. As you well know, Whitehall no longer holds a separate council meeting at the International Conference. In recent years they have called the International Council meeting to order in the context of large general sessions. They have not credentialed voting delegates but instead have taken perfunctory voice votes that have changed our constitution. This from an institution sanctimonious about high (and more, many more) standards of ethics.

I don't see how we can in good conscience call this latest review of our constitution an open dialogue. I don't see how we can characterize dialogue so carefully circumscribed as anything but regulated political speech. To argue that it was a well-intended attempt to provide a uniform structure to the debate in which every local, area and statewide Association addressed the same set of questions is nothing but bureaucratic doublespeak. It illustrates our international organization's penchant for bureaucratizing, one might just as easily say corporatizing, everything it touches—even if it means repudiating a long-standing tradition of autonomy and democratic process, even if it means taking an ethical stance that is so preoccupied with scandal that it lacks all sense of proportion. Whitehall's own ethics policy runs on for pages (you'd need an index to properly use it) with at least eighty standard statements at last count and a preamble that suggests more moral sanctimony to come. It is an ethical stance so overwrought that it positions us by extension to stand on ethical ground higher than any nonprofit in America. Saintly ground, as it were. But if we're obligated to be saints, we're almost certainly going to end up being sinners. Or as Orwell observed, it's not the difficulty in becoming a saint that puts people off; it's that they know they'll lose their humanity in the process. More rules and more standards might constrain some to act in a more punctilious way, but rules and standards will never elevate us to think and act in an admirable way, which has always been, since the time of the ancient Greeks, the true calling of an ethical life.

On a more practical level, Patrick, this burgeoning bureaucracy of standards is transforming us into a cookie-cutter, paint-by-the-numbers franchise that mindlessly roots out anything authentic and original in the local organizations. We are becoming, if we're not already there, inexorably, and I fear irreversibly, a corporate cliché. The accountability crowd in New York seems to believe that analytic overkill and the standardization it engenders will somehow coalesce into a Movement, into a Brand known for quality organizations and quality service. The irony is that it does just the opposite, deconstructing us into hundreds of parts or standards. I'm reminded of a comment that Hemingway made in a letter to his publisher, Charles Scribner, taking exception to some of the editorial suggestions for his novel, *For Whom the Bell Tolls.* "This book is one whole thing," he wrote, "not just a lot of parts." This is what we ought to strive to be, one whole thing, coalesced around a mission and a vision and no more than a few core principles. The rest should be left to us locals to experiment and innovate as serendipitously or as systematically as we please.

But the real constitutional question is not operational, tactical or strategic; it's structural. Our current constitution calls for us to govern but provides an inadequate structure to do it democratically. The International Council is so dysfunctional as a governing entity that it would be impossible to reform it in any substantive way. And Whitehall would fight fiercely to maintain its dominance and control of the Council anyway. Sadly, the Council has devolved into nothing more than a corporate annual meeting with all the brevity and expediency an annual meeting implies. I think we need an entirely new governing entity, which I'm calling a senate, which is still formulating in the irreverent mind of your old contrarian protégé, and about which I hope to have much to say later. Peace, my friend.

Corporate Philistinism

Anyone entering our homes should admire us rather than our furnishings.
~ Seneca

It's been a while since I sent you any news from the provinces out here on the western front, but much has happened since my last letter. We had a state Association meeting in Harrisburg the other day in which three International staffers came in from headquarters to do what they characterized as "training," though it might be more accurate to characterize what they did as getting our minds right. The first presentation was by a guy from the program department who came in to talk about getting kids engaged in community service. This topic really appealed to me because I think attending to the civic identities of kids—something which at least the public school system has largely abandoned—ought to be a primary preoccupation of a youth development agency like ours. But this was not to be any lesson on the merits of civic engagement. What this guy offered instead was a formula that Whitehall developed to calculate in numerical terms the value of community service conducted by our kids, which could then be used to attract corporate support. He had absolutely nothing to say about the intrinsic value of community service or other forms of civic engagement. He had nothing to say about the importance of democratic values in a democratic republic. There were no talking points from the founding, from the constitution, from the declaration, and you can forget about any references to classics like Tocqueville's *Democracy in America* or even an American classic like *The Federalist Papers*. That's what you get from the philistinism that comes from full-scale corporatization: community service understood as a number, as a meaningless metric.

If you think corporate philistinism is undermining the democratic project in America and in our Association, the descent is much more precipitous on matters of morality, of ethics, of what Whitehall calls public trust. Our second session at the state meeting was billed to be about ethics. One would expect Whitehall to send an ethicist to talk about ethics. They do in fact have on their letterhead the name of a reverend who is listed not just as a member of the International board but also as the board ethicist. But there was no reverend, no ethicist anywhere near this training session. Instead, they sent an accountant to lecture us about the importance of doing credit checks on our employees, because employees with bad credit ratings are more likely to be thieves. From there we were lectured about the importance of strengthening our whistleblower policy by providing potential whistleblowers with an anonymous 800 hotline. With that Orwellian thrust, I decided to tune out this otherwise affable, pot-bellied bean counter and get in a quick nap. I awoke near the end of the question and answer session. I raised my hand, not to ask a question, which, given the surveillance society commentary that preceded it, would have been a pointless exercise, but to make a point instead. I did this by invoking someone more appropriate for a discussion of ethics, the Roman philosopher Seneca. "Anyone entering our homes," I quoted Seneca as saying, "should admire us rather than our furnishings." You, I said to the bean counter, have offered us nothing but bad furnishings. I got in return a shrug, a bemused smile and a call for the next question.

Michael

A Constitution Revisited

...in a classic separation of powers.

Well, Patrick, on the international front, my complaining about Whitehall just having their hand-picked International Council Committee serve as the latest commission group has resulted in their appointing ten local executives to the commission. The Council Committee is made up of about twenty board volunteers from local Association organizations. I'm not sure how I was selected as one of the ten executives to serve on the commission. Perhaps the appointment came from Eileen Boyer. More likely it came from our old friend Denny McAndrew, who still manages the International Conference and has operational responsibility for organizational planning. Denny, as you well know, is quietly and carefully with us contrarians. How he has lasted at Whitehall the last twenty-five years is a mystery to me. I was lucky to last ten years there. Denny was one who encouraged me to go back to a local Association organization as an executive director. I remember him telling me that when you're an executive of one of the local organizations and you look over your shoulder, there's no one there. By contrast, when you look over your shoulder at headquarters, everybody above you in the bureaucracy is there watching.

Anyway, the commission will be meeting in

a couple of months. Denny, who is organizing the meeting, is already planning as part of the agenda to have one board volunteer and one local executive make an opening statement. Denny has already asked me to make the executive presentation to the commission which is now comprised of the twenty local board members from the Council Committee, the ten local executives, and several International board members, including the secretary of the international board, Anne Hopkins. I've started working on a paper I've tentatively titled *The Constitution Revisited.* The centerpiece of the paper will argue for the establishment of a senate to stand alongside the International Council, thus creating a bicameral form of governance. I don't think reforming the International Council, as some of our colleagues on the Cornell Crew have advised, would give us, the locals, any more control over our destiny than we now have. Even if we went back to the tradition of having a separate International Council Meeting with established quorums and credentialed delegates, this still leaves in place a structure that empowers the international organization to convene and set the agenda for the International Council. Our constitution clearly calls on us to govern but provides no real mechanism for us to do so. Our participation in this once democratic process constitutionally confers on us the legitimacy to govern. Whitehall has no such legitimacy. A senate would enable us to reclaim the legitimacy to govern the institution, conceding control of the Council to Whitehall while controlling the senate in a classic separation of powers.

Our Cornell Crew gets together well before the commission meets. If the Crew cannot be convinced that we need a new governance model, then in all probability the commission, and more importantly, the field, will not find it plausible either. Peace, Paddy. And give my love to Mary Margaret.

Remember, Michael, Whitehall isn't interested in changing course or reevaluating themselves based on thinking that comes from the field. It's all about process. It's an exercise. If they put you through the exercise, it doesn't matter if you call it a town hall meeting or a focus group, they have done all they need to do. This exercise is the means to justify the end that was decided before the exercise began. And you're right: now that they understand they can use the International Council as an instrument to get what they want, they will never relinquish control of it. As for all of us being sinners? Who would want to be anything but a sinner. See you in New York for the Cornell Crew Meeting.

The Bureaucratic Bane

Not only does power corrupt, as Lord Acton wisely observed, it consolidates itself around dull conformity and an ever expanding standardization.

You know, Patrick, we should probably find another venue to have our Crew meetings. Having the meetings in the northeast regional office means having to listen to the company clichés from our esteemed regional director. Your chairmanship of the Crew, my friend, created this practice of meeting at the home office and listening ad nauseam to this quintessential company man. David Wilson is otherwise a pretty nice guy, but put him in company mode and he is unreflectively insufferable. Luckily for us, Denny McAndrew was in town and was able to sit in and offer a more open viewpoint on the governance issue, a viewpoint that may or may not be shared by the big boss. My conversations with Eileen Boyer indicate a modest willingness to listen, but as of yet no inclination to support a specific change in our governance. I have no idea, for instance, what she thinks of the idea of creating a bicameral approach with the constitutional addition of a senate, other than her off-handed comment that it was an interesting idea.

You didn't miss anything in your absence; there was nothing at all interesting with what

David Wilson had to say last week as he regaled us with the current company line on the so-called vote to make the Standards, all 250 of them, a constitutional requirement of membership. His first line of attack was to say that funders are demanding greater compliance. Then he said that most local Associations want stricter brand compliance, followed by this platitudinous gem: we're only as good as our weakest link. Brand compliance? What fucking brand are we talking about? Walmart has a brand; they promise to give you the lowest price on any product you buy from them. You cannot brand something as nuanced as the emotional, physical and cognitive development of a child and therefore cannot reduce the larger meaning of humanity to corporate schlock.

And what David's reaction was when I asked him what our brand actually was? For a guy who can talk interminably about one prosaic matter after another, he was utterly confounded; he was, for the first and only time I can remember, speechless. He has, like many others in the Corporate State of America (forget United, who needs that lefty bullshit when one lives in the land of the free (enterprise) and the home of the (brand) used the term "brand" so long and so often it has become an archetypal, ineffable structure of meaning that doesn't lend itself to linguistic explanation. A brand, like the relativistic notion of art, quite simply, is. In that sense, everybody and every entity is a brand, an idea without content, a reputation only.

Leave it to our brilliant big bear of a friend from Jersey, Richard Norton, who always finds an opportunity at Cornell Crew meetings to take me to task, to come to the aid of the usually glib but now flummoxed David Wilson. Richard rather relishes taking me on, don't you think, Paddy? Despite initially agreeing that the governance system is broken, I thought he became quite disagreeable for the remainder of the meeting, particularly his insistence that the Standards that I've been railing against are what has enabled us to build a brand.

If we had a brand, one would have to point to our current tagline, the positive place for kids. As a building-centered youth agency, we are indeed a place, so the brand implication is that we're a safe place for kids. That may or may not be true. Many of our youth centers, particularly those in tough urban areas, are not for the faint of heart. There are some pretty tough kids in those places. Relatively speaking, these are safe places, but it's not the essence of who we are or what we do. You need to get to that essence if you're going to have a brand, then be able to bring that brand to the attention of various publics.

If we have a brand at all, I think it's the idea of making connections, lasting connections, deep connections between kids and caring adults. All of the great literature surrounding human development points to the fundamental need of every child to have a secure attachment to caring adults. To say that having hundreds of corporate standards in every conceivable category will ensure that these fundamental connections will be forged, is indeed, to borrow your term, an exercise—in idiocy. But Richard Norton is right in this respect, to pursue a brand you will be ineluctably drawn to a franchise-style standardization. It's the classic bureaucratic bane: not only does power corrupt, as Lord Acton wisely observed, it consolidates itself around dull conformity and an ever expanding standardization.

But I am encouraged that everybody at the meeting, with the exception of David Wilson, agreed that our governance model is broken. That includes Denny McAndrew who flippantly remarked that anything now put before the International Council—it could be something as silly as everybody must now wear hats—will pass without anyone really noticing. Denny also raised an interesting constitutional question when he suggested that it might be better to separate the international corporation from the federation, which is a radically different way of arriving at a bicameral structure. David Wilson probably got on the phone with Eileen immediately after the meeting to report on

Denny's heretical comments.

Other than sparring with David about the brand, much of what I said about constitutions might have been lost on the group. The main point I was trying to establish is that constitutions are designed to diffuse power not concentrate it. The corollary to this diffusion of power is the fact that constitutions are based not on standardized prescriptions but on general principles. But what we have already done, and continue to do, is turn a flawed but relatively sound constitutional document into one of corporate compliance. When we started working for this once venerable institution, my friend, the philistines were outside looking in. Now they're inside looking out at us, at their supine and disengaged focus group subjects. Maybe this mountain is too tall to climb. The next hillside on the horizon is my own board of directors. We're having a special meeting devoted entirely to the issue of governance and our place in it. Then I'm on to Dallas, to the big house for the big commission meeting. I'll keep you posted, Paddy.

Peace & Overthrow,
Michael

Restoring Democratic Governance

A senate, a true governing entity rather than a perfunctory meeting convened and controlled by the international organization, would give us the power to control our own destiny.

Meetings, Mr. McSweeney, the bane of any thinking nonprofit executive, have completely commanded my attention since I last wrote to you. There have been four meetings in all: two meetings of my board, a State Association meeting in Harrisburg, and a commission meeting at headquarters in Dallas. In each instance I was given the floor without any time constraints to make my case for adding a senate to our governance structure.

The first meeting was with my board and was devoted entirely to explaining the history and structure of the governance of this institution over the last century. My board volunteers came away with the understanding that the international entity of the Youth Association International has, unlike their businesses and professional entities but much like the local association organizations, a founding document, a constitution.

The Movement, then, as it is sometimes called, consists of two entities: the international organization (YAI), and the field, a federation of local member organizations like us, with the powers of each defined by a constitution that has undergone significant revision only in the last decade. In that sense, the constitution derives its authority and legitimacy from the consent of the governed, the consent of each local Association member. We, the local organizations, the actual voting members, are the governing entity, and that governance used to be exercised through our full engagement in the International Council.

The international organization, which is not a voting member, is simply the executive entity responsible for holding local organizations accountable to the general membership provisions of the constitution.

The state associations, a late addition to the constitution and structure of the organization, were originally created to provide training and discussion opportunities for board volunteers. They have since devolved into entities designed to lobby state governments for funding. It is these state associations, I explained, that would become the mechanism for creating a senate, a governance structure that would have two senators from each State Association.

At the State Association Meeting, where representatives from the Pennsylvania organizations have already heard me comment on the diminution of democratic governance that has occurred during Eileen Boyer's tenure as international president, I concentrated on the reasons why we need a senate.

I first of all argued that our current governance structure, or what passes for it, the International Council, calls on the field to govern but does not provide an adequate framework to exercise that governance effectively or democratically. An International Senate, standing alongside the International Council, would enable us to govern—thoughtfully, deliberatively, democratically.

The fundamental democratic tenet of the International Senate, which would have two representatives from every state, area or territorial association, is that no measure could become part of our constitution unless it passed the truest democratic test: the support of a majority of the organizations in our Movement, thus ending, at least technically, the-majority-of-a-minority rule based upon a twenty-five percent quorum (though Whitehall has not really counted any votes or kept any records in at least a decade).

The senate also would enable the field to stand on an international stage on which local organizations could communicate and have dialogue and debate across area, regional and national lines.

It would enable us to do our own convening, presiding and agenda-setting.

We could counter or support, as the case may be, matters brought before the International Council.

The senate, a true governing entity rather than a perfunctory annual meeting convened and controlled by the international organization, would give us the power to control our destiny; it would provide a legitimate framework for real democratic engagement on the part of the field.

I concluded my comments to the State Association by saying that it would be politically naïve to graft the senate model onto the existing International Council. This would require wresting control of our governance from Whitehall, a state of affairs which Whitehall would never allow, thus leaving our international organization in complete control of our governance.

My final comment was that our constitution called on us to govern. It rested the real power and legitimacy of our Movement in us, in the consent of the governed. It's time to exercise that power, I said, wisely and democratically.

After this somewhat impassioned plea, a motion was made to support the establishment of a senate as a way of restoring democratic governance. It passed unanimously without a contrary comment. It is now known as The Pennsylvania Proposal.

Michael

Calling The Corporate Question

We should never think of ourselves as shareholders in a corporation. We should instead think of ourselves as owners of a democratically constituted federation.

Dallas was a different matter, Patrick. It was a larger group, about fifty people, crammed in a basement room that could comfortably accommodate about thirty people. Instead of sitting at a hollow square facing each other, we were seated theater style. I ended up, as I did in my school days, in the back of the room. Whereas I knew almost all of the people at the state meeting and they had heard me talk on the subject of governance before, only a few people at the commission meeting, mostly national board members, knew who I was, and no one in the room, other than Denny McAndrew, who was facilitating the meeting, had any idea of what I was about to say. The room was so crowded that when Denny called on me to, as he said, say a few words, I simply stood up in the back of the room and said many more words than anyone expected.

What I actually did was read from the paper I'd written for the occasion called "The Constitution Revisited." I made all of the major arguments I made to my board and to the folks from the State Association. I noted that in the last decade the powers of the Council have been diminished while those of the international organization have been enhanced; that now the national board, not the Council membership, elects the officers of the Council, and the Council no longer has the power to appoint members to the national board. I noted the mysterious appearance of the term "operating standards" in our constitution and its implications for having our constitution regarded as a prescriptive compliance document rather than a general framework for governance. I also wondered if there were records that could tell us when these votes were taken, what local organizations actually constituted the quorum, and what organizations actually voted for all these constitutional changes. I mentioned that their most recent town hall meetings were nothing more than an exercise in regulated political speech and that the overreaction to scandal that prompted them ultimately pushed us into an ethical stance that lacks all sense of proportion. Ethics, I said, is not a laundry list of regulatory prescriptions. Ethics elevates; it edifies; it is a view of the higher life that inspired our vision for the young people we serve, a vision to lift whole generations of young people to a level of civic engagement not seen since the founding of our nation. And so on.

The opening paragraphs of the paper, which I've left for last, gave an historical and philosophical context to the argument that I had never voiced to anyone or any group before. Here it is in its entirety.

James Madison, writing in *The Federalist Papers,* described our country's constitution as an imperfect document. If Madison and the other architects of the world's most admired constitution could only produce a magnificent imperfection, I think we can agree that our own constitution is neither perfect nor magnificent. Its primary imperfection is that it is actually an uneven amalgam of two constitutional models—one corporate, one political.

The corporate part of the constitution, which has emerged largely in the last decade, is a vertically integrated model that derives its authority and legitimacy from those who govern (international board members) and those delegated to govern (international staff). Its locus of power and authority is at and near the top. It is by definition top down.

By contrast, the historic and original political structure of our constitution is a horizontally decentralized federation that derives its power and legitimacy—much like the U.S. Constitution—from the consent of the governed, from the consent of each individual Youth Association organization. This part of our governance, which has been in rapid decline over the last decade and has all but disappeared, is bottom up.

So we now have two entities with no definitive separation of powers and no clear mechanism, as in the case of the U.S. Constitution, for one entity to check the over-reaching of the other. We have instead an executive branch that convenes, sets the agenda, and purportedly counts the votes and keeps the records for the legislative branch and a legislative branch that elects the governing body (the International Association's board volunteers) of the executive branch. In a constitutional structure in which a separation of powers prevailed, one would think that the legislative branch would do its own convening and presiding and agenda-setting and the executive branch would elect, appoint or otherwise choose its own members.

There are essentially three ways, I told the commission members, to resolve this dichotomy. One is to become a single unified corporation under the command and control of headquarters in Dallas. The other is to empower the field to govern democratically by majority consensus rather than minority rule. The third way is to share power by establishing a bicameral governance structure in which a senate (which, I added, the Pennsylvania Association unanimously endorsed) would operate under the aegis of the field and a council under the aegis of the international organization.

When I finished talking, I noticed that the room was completely silent. Anne Hopkins, the secretary of the international board, a rather congenial New York socialite with just the slightest hint of an Upper East Side manner, finally spoke, at first addressing me directly. "Thank you, Michael. Your remarks were very impressive from an intellectual and philosophical standpoint, but"—then turning to Denny McAndrew who was standing near her at the front of the room, she said—"Denny, would you mind correcting the errors in Michael's remarks?" I knew from the pained expression on Denny's wizened, shadow-bearded face that he had indeed heard what Anne Hopkins asked him to do, but instead of acknowledging her he simply introduced the next item on the meeting agenda. And with no further discussion of my remarks, of what has become known as The Pennsylvania Proposal, I have no idea of what the commission members thought of it.

After I got back from Harrisburg and Dallas, my board met again and unanimously decided to request that a proposal to establish a senate be placed on the agenda of the International Council Meeting next year in San Diego. The letter was addressed, as Denny McAndrew advised us to do, to the secretary of the International Board of Directors, Anne Hopkins, and signed by me and my board president.

We noted in our letter that the senate idea had the unanimous support of our State

Association, and we made it clear that the senate was not being proposed as a replacement of the International Council, but rather an addition to it, thus creating a bicameral governance structure. We also made it clear that the senate, unlike the International Council, would be a representative policy-making body through which all constitutional revisions would have to pass. The letter concluded by explaining that each state association would have two senators, one a local association executive and the other a local board volunteer. The senate would meet at least bi-annually, elect its own officers, provide for an appropriate committee structure, and, although the international organization would have two senators to represent them, the convening, presiding and agenda-setting would be under the auspices of the senate.

What this democratic front comes down to is the notion that nonprofits should be defined by the constitutional premise that power ought to be shared and balanced; it ought to be diffused rather than concentrated at the top as it is in almost all corporations. We should never think of ourselves as shareholders in a corporation, as our regional director continually calls us. We should instead think of ourselves as owners of a democratically-constituted federation. Well, we have, as you like to say, called the question. Whitehall can either concur or fight. I guess we'll soon see.

Michael

Michael, my boy, two things, one seemingly small, the other obviously big. Your wondering, as you put it, about whether there are records of Council meetings from the last decade or so seems small and insignificant, but it's really a huge problem for them. If they can't produce those records, you know, quorums and votes, then all of the constitutional amendments they pushed through while no one was paying attention are invalid. What they've done is at least unethical if not illegal. It's a big problem for them. Your mentioning it in front of a fifty-person commission—in effect a national audience—had to scare the hell out of them. Maybe that was one of the errors that Anne Hopkins wanted Denny to correct.

The big one, which we've talked about many times, and which you may or may not have mentioned, is the fact that over the last two decades Whitehall, while getting tens of millions of dollars from the federales, has become an ongoing funder of local organizations. This has completely corrupted our politics, our democratic norms, as you like to call them. No organization receiving grant money from Whitehall is going to vote against them on any matter, big or small. Without fixing that, there are no democratic norms, no democratic institution, no democracy. As our friend Doug Hays likes to say, money talks and bullshit walks. They've got the money, and all we've got, however good it might be, is the good stuff, the true stuff, the, well, bullshit.

The Darwinian Field and its Babbitt-like Bustle

We shyly wish to live by our eyes and our wits,
at our desks, away from the broad brawl,
to give it a name, of salesmanship.
~ John Updike

You know, Patrick, if we could get a senate in place, we'd have the platform and the power—yes, I'm afraid that politics at its essence is about little more than the naked exercise of power—to take on the issue you like to call "the big one," which is of course that incandescently unethical conflict of interest by which Whitehall pays, in the form of grants, the entities that vote on the policies and procedures and standards Whitehall wants in place. Even if one member organization—and I'm pretty sure there are many—refuses to vote a certain way for fear of losing funding from Whitehall, the governance of the entire institution is ethically compromised.

This conflict does not even register with them despite all the discoursing on ethics and public trust. It doesn't register because in this decades-long descent into corporate expediency, the democratic idea of casting votes has become utterly quaint and superfluous, not to mention messy and inefficient. This facile philistinism is emblematic of the kind of thinking corporatism spawns, thinking that is simplistic, formulaic, phony, and not in any real sense broad or deep or fundamentally curious. Our business brothers—and now most of our executives are business types with no breadth or depth in the humanities—would have us believe that strategic thinking, about which most of them only have the fuzziest understanding, is somehow deep, broad, meaningful.

For the philistines among us—now, sadly, a relatively youthful and callow majority—the idea that a nonprofit institution such as ours has only instrumental value is a fervently-held business belief. It is the idea that our institution is only a means to solving social problems and not, even in part, an end in itself. But if we thought more deeply about this matter and understood that our institution had intrinsic as well as instrumental value, then we could see its value as a democratic institution in which power is diffused rather than concentrated. After all, democratic states need democratic institutions. We were able to form a democratic republic in 1787 largely because democratic institutions had flourished in the colonies for the better part of two centuries. The most pressing danger to democratic life in America, aside from the plutocratic cosmos that cynically sees corporations as people and money as speech, is at the quantum level, in the many varied institutions in towns and cities across America, where the corporate model is king and the democratic institution a vanquished vassal.

It may be that this love of the humanities on our part is as much snobbish as it is defeatist. I cannot help believing that if our organization had recruited the coming generation, those in their thirties and forties, say, from the ranks of the liberal arts instead of the business world, so that our executives would actually be knowledgeable about what's fundamentally important to the children we're trying to nurture, we would have had the intellectual resources to resist the coarse corporatizing of our institution. A novelist like Updike says in his memoirs that people like us have been marginalized, that we "shyly wish too live by our eyes and our wits, at our desks, away from ... the broad brawl, to give it a name, of salesmanship." For that is the world of our old friend, Eileen Boyer, the "broad brawl," the Darwinian field on which we must fight against other sellers and sound biters to sell our service to anyone who will pay for it. From our perch one could say we're looking down on this Babbit-like bustle, but with the ground on which we stand about to completely crumble, we will, when this corporatization is complete, be looking up at these Babbits, badly beaten.

A postscript, Paddy. That now rare American man of letters and pride of Shillington, Pennsylvania, the late John Updike, once wrote that "Sun and moon, sun and moon, time goes," and oh how it does indeed go, though in the world that Einstein dispensed to us it might be more apt to say that we move through time given that time and space are weirdly conjoined. My most recent movement was through another Denny McAndrew conference, through another fly-by, two-minute International Council Meeting self-confidently presided over by that Tom Wolfean Master of the Universe, Steve Davis, who, I'm ecstatic to note, announced that the Pennsylvania Proposal has been formally submitted for consideration by the International Council. This means, as you know, that our proposed senate will be voted up or down at next year's conference. And since nothing brought before the Council in almost two decades has been voted down, Whitehall is in the extraordinarily awkward position of orchestrating the first and only no-vote in Eileen's entire tenure as CEO. Win or lose—and winning for the moment seems sadly remote—it will be a joy to watch what they come up with, which I presume will be nothing short of political prestidigitation.

And I will see you, my good man, at the Cornell Crew Meeting among Melville's Manhattoe s, at which time we will discuss and debate, among other things, a book about how nonprofits ought to be able to use all the tools of capitalism to properly fight society's ills.

2

The Decline and Fall of Charity

One of the most striking tendencies of our time is the expansion of markets and market-oriented reasoning into spheres of life traditionally governed by non-market norms.
~ Michael Sandel

The Nonprofit as Economic Entity

Nonprofits, after decades of relentless corporatization, have become little more than capitalist tools.

I guess Peter Siegel wasn't exactly enamored with what I had to say about Dan Pallotta's book at our Cornell Crew meeting. It was Peter, after having heard Pallotta speak at a Chamber of Commerce event, who suggested we put the book on the agenda of our Cornell Crew meeting. Well, it wasn't really Pallotta's book Peter wanted on the agenda; it was Pallotta's speech, which argued, among other corporate gems, that nonprofit executives ought to be paid commensurate to the kind of colossal compensation now commonplace in corporate America. Our boy Peter likes the idea of being paid the big bucks to pick the pockets of corporate America. That's not the part of the job of executive director, or in today's corporate lingo, chief professional officer, that I particularly like. I know you're not with me on this, Patrick; you rather enjoyed the challenge of raising money from corporations.

My favorite contemporary essayist, however, one Joseph Epstein, whom *The Boston Globe* called both elegantly charming and curmudgeonly mordant, is with me on this one. Epstein, an intellectual type, a humanities man who came out of the University of Chicago and Northwestern, a guy generally conservative in his politics but perfectly comfortable with the idea of living the life of the mind, remarked in one of his essays that there are some jobs distinctly not worth having like proctologist and any job that requires sucking up to the rich. I take this to mean that sucking up to the rich, which Peter and others are willingly disposed to do for a six-figure salaries and various other compensation package perks, is the equivalent of peering into the dark world of anal cavities. It is, at least figuratively, then, asshole work.

But Pallotta's book is, if nothing else, bold. He certainly asks the right question: To what extent should nonprofits operate like corporations? That may be the right question, but his overall answer I find hard to fathom: capitalism, as it relates to the effectiveness and purpose of nonprofits, is not the problem; the lack of it is. His thesis, which also happens to be the subtitle of his book, is that restraints on nonprofits undermine their potential.

It is, as I say, a pretty bold vision, one that envisions a nonprofit world capable of achieving Apollo-level results, like ending poverty, not just ameliorating it, but ending it, in ten years, mind you. That is certainly thinking big, but not nearly as bold as Pallotta would like us to believe, given that nonprofits, after decades of relentless corporatization, have become little more than capitalist tools. His prescription for the future of nonprofits vastly underestimates the extent to which nonprofits already function as corporations. Nonprofits are just not sufficiently capitalistic to satisfy Pallotta's libertarian worldview, a view that comes right from the pages of Ayn Rand's *The Virtue of Selfishness.*

Pallotta seems to want to do good—solve poverty, for example—without having any conception of the common good. His Randian individualism may indeed fuel more wealth formation in the nonprofit world—though, as you well know, many nonprofits already have huge endowments and ample amounts of cash on their balance sheets—but it would effectively end the idea that nonprofits are something more than economic entities whose purpose is nothing more than to raise money to solve social problems like poverty and AIDS.

In Pallotta's worldview, there is no intrinsic value to nonprofit institutions; they're simply a means to solving social problems, not ends in themselves. He has no civic sense of nonprofits as democratic institutions that build social capital, as social institutions led by people who know something other than the meaning of money and the power of advertising and are paid an amount commensurate to that of the staff members they lead.

Michael

Executive Compensation

So we should benchmark executive compensation for nonprofit executives to these modern American Robber Barons?

This whole matter of executive compensation, Paddy, is pretty revealing when you've got guy like Pallotta, in this new Gilded Age of corporate executives making tens of millions of dollars, an ever widening economic inequality, a declining middle class, poverty rising rapidly, and here he is carping about the fact—at least he calls it a fact—that corporate executives make thirty times more than nonprofit execs. So we should benchmark executive compensation for nonprofit execs to these Robber Barons? And we should do this, he argues, because it is the only way to attract top executive talent capable of raising the big bucks which would then be applied to solving the big problems? This is a guy who at one point in his book quotes Oscar Wilde as defining a cynic as one who knows the cost of everything and the value of nothing. From a guy who sees money as the maker of all things good, bringing up Wilde in this context is so lacking in self-awareness that it stumbles into the delusional.

Setting aside for a moment the view of Jim Collins, the most notable business writer in America, that the best executives will come out of the nonprofit world, I think there is another good reason to challenge Pallotta's defense of colossal compensation for nonprofit executives. What Pallotta does not report is the widening disparity between executive compensation and the amounts paid to entry-level and mid-level nonprofit employees. It's not uncommon even in our own field to see execs from fairly large organizations making, say, $150,000 per year, while the entry level jobs start at less than $20,000 per year. I'm sure this disparity is much wider in the corporate world, but as we become more corporatized and become more inclined to adopt the philosophy Pallotta is espousing, the equity gap will only grow. Clearly, Pallotta, a former nonprofit executive himself, wants to get his, and wants us, like his Robber Baron buddies, to get ours.

Michael

Leadership and the Youth Agency Executive

Is it desirable to hire people to lead our agencies who know nothing about human development, but who know the difference between a budget and a balance sheet?

But it isn't just pay, Patrick, that is a problem with Pallotta's program for executive leadership; it's that he takes it as a given, as conventional wisdom, to use a term he disingenuously borrows from the great liberal economist John Kenneth Galbraith, that nonprofit leadership should come from America's business schools or from the business world in general. For our purposes, as a youth development agency, this means that it is not only all right but it is desirable to hire people to lead our agencies who know nothing about human development or child development, who wouldn't know Rousseau from Locke, Erickson from Freud, Bolby from Bandura, but who do know the difference between a budget and a balance sheet. Peter Siegel and others on our Cornell Crew have, after multiple manhattans, made this same argument to me. What do we, as youth development agency executives, need to know about the soul and psychology of the children we serve? Nothing, apparently, not one fucking thing. We can, and should, as their argument goes, hire other people to take care of that insignificant stuff. What other people, I ask? Kids coming out of college with degrees in criminal justice or communications or business—or even education for that matter—know precious little about the dimensions of childhood. This is precisely the corporate climate that leaves us vulnerable to virtually every business bromide ever conceived by the Captains of Industry, from quality standards to outcomes measurement, a vulnerability that will grow worse unless we can reverse the trend and find a way to attract bright people liberally educated in the humanities. This of course assumes that such a cohort of educated people still exists in America today. Sadly, I don't think that it does.

Galbraith in Context

The point Galbraith was setting up was not that we needed an unrestrained all-out expansion of capitalism... but a public policy focused on the public good.

You know, Patrick, Pallotta made a mockery of one of the great intellectuals of the twentieth century, liberally quoting Galbraith out of context to make claims with which Galbraith would have been utterly horrified. This is intellectual dishonesty of the most egregious sort. At the conclusion of his chapter on the influence of Puritanism on today's charitable assumptions, Pallotta observes that Puritan beliefs are not as extreme as they once were, but "they have not been fundamentally transformed. There has been no movement toward the rejection of self-sacrifice as the road to social change." A few paragraphs later, he quotes Galbraith from *The Affluent Society:* "The affluent country which conducts its affairs in accordance with rules of another and poorer age also foregoes opportunities." In context, Galbraith's remark had nothing at all to do with Puritanism or the idea of self-sacrifice. Galbraith was simply setting up his general thesis that some modern nations like the United States are no longer societies in which the majority of people live in poverty and that we should no longer be bound by the ideas that came out of this world of "grim scarcity." The point Galbraith was setting up was not that we needed an unrestrained, all-out expansion of capitalism of the kind that Pallotta is promoting for the nonprofit world, but rather a public policy that focused on the public good rather than the production of private goods, a public policy that—if we were ever to solve the problem of poverty—would require a "massively greater investment in the public sector."

On the issue of advertising, Pallotta goes even further afield to make another disingenuous connection to Galbraith. Pallotta's point is that if we applied the lessons of mass advertising to nonprofits, we would get a geometric increase in donations. Advertise more, people will give more; ad campaigns in the millions will raise charitable dollars in the hundreds of millions, even billions. Conceding that Galbraith is writing about "services provided by the government to meet social needs," Pallotta offers up this quote from *The Affluent Society* as he pushes his point about the advisability, the necessity really, of greatly expanding nonprofit advertising:

> While public services have been subject to these negative attitudes, private goods have had no such attention. On the contrary, their virtues have been extolled by the massed drums of modern advertising…The social consequences of this discrimination—this tendency to accord superior prestige to

> private goods and an inferior role to public production—are considerable and even grave.

If you hadn't read Galbraith—and no one, other than you and I, on the Cornell Crew has read him, and probably almost no one in our entire field—you wouldn't know that Galbraith would never conclude from these remarks that we need massive amounts of additional advertising, even for public services. Put in context, the argument that Galbraith is actually making in the above quote is for greater acceptance of taxation to fund public projects for the common good. It doesn't matter to Pallotta if Galbraith believes that advertising manufactures wants that were not there to begin with and are not meaningful once they are. For unrepentant philistines like Pallotta, if more advertising means more money for nonprofits to solve social problems, then more advertising it is. In my county alone there are about five hundred nonprofit organizations all seeking the attention of various publics, and none of these publics—whether they are corporations, foundations, governmental entities, united ways or individuals—can readily and confidently tell one nonprofit from another. These publics are already exhausted from the informational bombardment coming from nonprofits.

Michael

Picking pockets, Palermo? What's wrong with that? As long as it's the pockets of, as you like to call them, the Robber Barons. All you can really do is play the game, and if you play it well, you win. Everybody wins. That's all that really matters. And you're right, this Pallotta guy has largely missed how much nonprofits have already become, mostly in the last thirty years or so, as you like to call it, corporate clichés. Where we haven't quite gone yet, except for the big boys in higher ed and health care, is big-time capital formation of the kind that Pallotta is promoting. He makes a point when he argues that organizations with a higher overhead are more effective than those with lower overhead costs; that this whole emphasis on efficiency, as measured by overhead costs, means that the nonprofit world will never be more than marginally effective in solving social problems. We will never be, in other words, sufficiently capitalized to solve big problems long-term.

Look at our organization. The combined budgets of all of our local Associations is somewhere in the neighborhood of eight-hundred million. Let's say it's an even billion. Don't you think with, say, two billion, we could do something really transformative? To your point, we could, with that kind of money, attract the best and the brightest to work for our organizations instead of just getting by with poorly-paid part-timers.

But maybe more money just won't get it done, Michael. Look at Lyndon Johnson, a man who understood power, a political genius of the first rank, who, with the power and resources of the federal government for his War on Poverty, couldn't get it done. Poverty is as bad as it's ever been. And this guy, this Don Quixote of the nonprofit version of the capitalist class, he's going to solve poverty and cure AIDS by turning these issues over to a completely corporatized nonprofit sector? However unregulated and unrestrained the nonprofit sector becomes, it will never come close to cobbling together even a piddling percentage of what the federal government can and already has brought to bear. Not a snowballs chance.

Agency Overhead and Efficiency Fraud

The approach to agency overhead now taken by charities and auditing firms alike is a fraud of formidable proportions.

Speaking of LBJ, that old scamp and political intriguer was never anything close to being a Captain of Industry (try teacher and school principal) before becoming what our betters would regard as at least a near-great twentieth-century president. George W. Bush and Herbert Hoover were the business boys who rose to the presidency in the last century, and neither one would make anyone's list of great or near-great presidents. Truman would rank high, but he dropped out of business school after one semester and his haberdashery shop went bankrupt. So I say let the business boys (and girls) be in business and take their business bromides with them. What we need in our field are leaders with good judgment, with an education that is as broad as it is deep, and with a little bit of wisdom about the world in general and the nonprofit world in particular. To do otherwise would, as Galbraith observed, have us forever moored to "a firm anchor in nonsense." Not surprisingly, Peter Siegel's Man of Much More Than LaMancha used the "anchor in nonsense" metaphor to make another non-Galbraithian point, this time concerning the legacy of Puritanism's anti-self interest ideology. Galbraith made the comment in an entirely different context to discredit the idea of promoting production by contriving wants.

As for the efficiency argument, sure, you would expect more money, much more in the scenario you have laid out, to conduce to a higher quality guidance and youth development experience for the kids who come to our centers. The problem with this argument is that it's a disingenuous attempt to have it both ways: have higher capitalization like the corporate world Pallotta wants to emulate but without the efficiency of operation that competitive capitalism routinely requires. Even if you accept the assumption that nonprofits in general need to be more fully capitalized—i.e., they need to raise geometrically more money—then you have to ask, how much is enough? How much is too much? Or is it just the more the merrier? And if you're the donor giving the money or the funder providing the funds, how do you decide who to give your money to while you wait out the decade it will take for the agency or agencies you support to end poverty or cure AIDS? How do you compare the quality of one agency against another? If you're the individual or entity providing the money to the nonprofit(s), then it would be circuitous and self-serving logic to use money as your measure of quality.

Pallotta'a plausible answer is that if we "measure business by the bottom line," then the "bottom line for charity is effectiveness." He quickly concedes, and rightly so, that agency effectiveness is "more difficult to measure than corporate profits" and is not something you can distill down "to a single metric." So what are his metrics? What a wonderful term—metrics! It goes so well with money and marketing to make for a kind of holy trinity, a 3M of eternal verities for the corporate culture of charity: money, marketing and metrics.

Pallotta's metrics, his measures of effectiveness, include some rather odd and some pretty pedestrian things, like the effectiveness of a charity's programs, the quality of the staff, how clients rate the charity's efforts, the incremental effect of a donation in the present moment (whatever that means), how well-known the charity is to the public (general? other publics?), the effect of economic conditions on the charity, comparisons to other charities of a similar kind, intangible benefits (?), the value of the outcome, bold initiatives, long-term vision, long-term investments effect on short-term finances, and adequate infrastructure. Many of these so-called metrics—program effectiveness, client ratings, public awareness, the value of the services to the community, and a strategic vision statement—are already widely used by most charities and the entities that fund them.

What's new about Pallotta's approach is that he would create what he calls a "state-of-the-art assessment apparatus" (nice technological tone to this cliché), "something magnificent," with "an army (another nice big money metaphor) of exceptional people (soldiers?) with exceptional technology (apparatuses must be, one would think, technologically advanced) and leadership (you gotta have leadership, the condiment that accompanies all human endeavors)—an organization situated across the nation, where our charities actually operate" (where else?). And from the deployment of this army of professional auditors, "teams of specialists" (is there anything else?) will "perform a many-faceted audit" on presumably all of the charities in America, to be paid for by taking one-half of one percent of all contributions to charity in a given year. If that number were roughly 295 billion, then you'd have about 1.475 billion to pay for all the apparatuses. Well, not quite that much, because you'd have to "assume a management and general rate of 30 percent off of (really bad grammar) that total," leaving about 1.03 billion "for assessment."

For a Randian libertarian and a Milton Friedman free-market capitalist, this guy has a rather bureaucratic statist approach to evaluating charities. At least he would make the donors, not the taxpayers, pay for throwing another billion dollars to the auditing franchise. And it would, in my view, end up under the aegis of the auditing crowd, since they already own the franchise and have enough influence with the Captains of Industry to make certain that they also would own and operate the apparatus that Pallotta envisions. You'd think a guy with his capitalist bona fides would conjure up a more flexible, decentralized, community-based approach to evaluating charities.

Pallotta's approach, by contrast, "would involve teams of data-gathering analysts" (ah, data, the mustard to leadership's ketchup) who "would conduct face-to-face meetings (the anti technology phase), tours of facilities, surveys of clients, surveys of donors, surveys of financial information (How about some Gallup Polls to pick up a little trend data?), analysis (plenty of analysis, I'm sure, from battalions and brigades of accountant-like analysts) of long-term plans, infrastructure planning, and conversations about needs and dreams (no Freudian dream analysis, I'm sure). It gets worse: The armies of analysts then "would compile their information (data sounds better, more post-modern) according to consistent formats that could easily be sorted and perused online with extremely user-friendly interfaces." Then this: "A user (How about a peruser/donor/funder with nothing better to do?) could flip online (or is it flip out?) through a variety of client testimonials, candid staff comments (good luck with that), comments from other donors, and financial metrics ranging over a period of years, not months." Finally, this from a guy named Tinkelman from a publication called "Research in Government and Nonprofit Accounting" on how to judge the effectiveness of a charity: "we really want to examine the number of units of high quality charitable outputs per dollar donated to the cause." To borrow a vaudevillian punch-line from our late B-Movie Actor-in-Chief, there you go again, with all those financial metrics and outputs per dollar donated, reaffirming, as if it ever needed reaffirming, that it is indeed a small, small apparatus world.

But then again one would have to concede that the approach to agency overhead now taken by charities and auditing firms alike is a fraud of formidable proportions. Pallotta pointed to the "Nonprofit Overhead Cost Project" which studied the 990's of over one hundred thousand charities and found that half of small charities (revenues less than a million) reported no fundraising expenses at all, and of the larger charities (one to five million) a full quarter of them also reported having no fundraising expenses whatsoever. The real scam occurs, as you well know, when the field auditors ask nonprofit executives and other management and fundraising staff how much time they spend on program. An old colleague of ours once told an auditor that he spent absolutely no time at all on program, if, as he explained, the definition of program is time spent working directly with agency clients. The auditor, I am told, turned ashen from what must have been a data-deprived anxiety attack and said, anxiously but emphatically, "You can't do that."

"Why not?"

"Because it's not true. You must spend some time on program-related matters. Meetings, reports. That kind of thing."

"That kind of thing is not program," said our truth-telling friend.

Bug-eyed with panic, this newly minted CPA and associate in training (it should be CBC, certified bean counter), authoritatively announced, "You simply cannot do that!"

"Yes I can," our brave brother said, though not really serious, just teasing, while the auditor riffled through the bean file from the previous year's audit, finally tapping the relevant bean and announcing with renewed vigor: "Last year we had you down for fifty-five percent management and forty-five percent program. We can't very well put down one hundred percent management for this year."

I'm told it ended up being fifty-five forty-five, which, as we all know, is how the game is played. That's how all of our Cornell Crew colleagues can publish an annual report in which ninety percent or more of their revenues are attributed to program, a fraudulent statistic certified by the impressive-sounding title of some buttoned-down, lily-white, almost all-male accounting firm. That's enough for now, Patrick. I think my reservoir of irony and disdain has, for the moment at least, run dry. Ciao.

Yes, it looks like our Don Quixote from the land of Rand has brought out the ironist in you. But it's okay to be a little pissed off. It'll keep you fired up for the coming fight with the folks at Whitehall. You're going to need a lot of that if we're ever to wrest political control of the institution from what you like to call the philistines. If the rest of the world is going to hell in a corporate hand-basket, there is at least some hope, a little glimmer perhaps, of keeping this one charitable institution in the democratic column. You have to keep fighting, Michael, keep believing, that we're going to win.

Charity as Quid Pro Quo

We have conflated patronage, in which a donor's support is given in exchange for something, with true charity, which is freely given.

Patrick, I haven't forgotten our last exchange and your exhortation concerning the coming fight with Whitehall. The conference and the vote on our senate proposal, which I keep calling The Pennsylvania Proposal, but which Whitehall, even our friend behind the lines, Denny McAndrew, keeps referring to as The Erie Proposal, is now only a month away. There hasn't been any politicking on this vote by either side, the result of a non-aggression pact between me and Eileen Boyer that Denny deftly negotiated. So I'm going into the International Council Meeting not knowing what to expect. Denny and I haven't talked lately, but I'm assuming that I'll have an opportunity to speak before the vote is taken, for which I've prepared three possible presentations: a two-minute, a five-minute, and if it's looking rather bleak, a ten-minute philippic denouncing the corporatization of our institution and of virtually every other province of American life, including the bigger province into which our once-democratic institution fits, that of charity.

In some ways it is more lamentable to look at what has happened to the idea of charity in general. Pallotta's take on the Puritans is that their self-sacrificial ideology has constrained the modern nonprofit from achieving greater impact that could have and should have been achieved by imitating the successes (greater capital formation) and excesses (exorbitant executive compensation) of corporate culture. If the donor world actually saw charity in self-sacrificial terms, Pallotta might have a more powerful point. It is, after all, the donor that ultimately determines the success or failure of nonprofits, if one defines success, as Pallotta does, as raising big sums of money to solve big problems. But I think it's rather dubious that the donor really gives a damn about efficiency, as Pallotta has posited. They do, however, care about what they're getting for their contribution. Charity is now conceived of as a quid pro quo. What we have done is allow a materialistic business culture to define charity down to an act of patronage. We have conflated patronage, in which a donor's support is given in exchange for something (name recognition, a quantifiable outcome, an award), with true charity, which is freely given. Even a business writer like Jim Collins has questioned the legitimacy of donors commanding, in many cases demanding, something in return for their donation. My view is that if charity cannot function in its truest sense and be freely given without conditions or qualifications, without expectations of getting something in return, and is instead reduced to a business transaction, then it should not be allowed as a charitable deduction and it should not have the moral stature of charity. True charity elevates the soul of the giver and enriches the well-being of the receiver, but charity thanked is charity diminished, and charity immortalized is charity undone.

This loss of the moral and spiritual nature of charity is the more important historical connection we should make with Puritans like John Winthrop, who said in his famous sermon "A Model of Christian Charity," that "wee must be knit together in this worke as one man, wee must entertaine each other in brother Affeccion, we must be willing to abridge our selves of our superfluities, for the supply of others' necessities…" Whereas Pallotta, the radical individualist, can only see self-sacrifice in Winthrop's sentiment, he misses entirely the idea that individual selves can and should accommodate themselves to a common purpose, a common good, "a worke as one man," without a fundamental diminution of self. Even the Darwinian-driven Robber Baron ought to be able to give to charity without expecting a return on his investment or experiencing some sense of self diminishment. The problem is that the American citizen, as Tocqueville pointed out nearly two centuries ago, "is habitually busy with the contemplation of a very petty object, which is himself." Or as Allan Bloom put it just a quarter of a century ago, "People don't reason beyond the calculation of self-interest."

Michael

Professionalized Charity

Philanthropy, as opposed to charity,
sacrificed its moral purpose.
~Robert Gross

The approach that Pallotta has taken, Paddy, aside from its concerns about self-sacrifice, is, in economic terms, relentlessly and unapologetically capitalistic, reminding me of an observation by C. Wright Mills, that "prosperity, however unequally distributed" (and it is about unequal as it has ever been), "presents itself as the all-purpose solution to all social questions." A position certainly similar to, if not identical to, the serially misquoted John Kenneth Galbraith.

Charity started out, in 17th and 18th century America, having both a spiritual and a personal dimension. Traditional charity of the kind apportioned in Winthrop's Bay Colony was not only alms for the poor but also took the form of, as Robert Gross has written, "good advice, a kind word, or an exhortation to piety." Like the charity dispensed in the New England town or the New York or Virginia parish vestry, "every community established in the Bay Colony was obligated to take care of its own legal inhabitants" so that "aid to the needy was direct, personal, concrete" (Gross). The poor were not given money to spend as they desired, but instead were given things like food and clothing and firewood, "a distribution that followed the Marxist formula quite literally: from each according to his ability, to each according to his needs" (Gross).

Now wouldn't that please our betters, Patrick, to know that charity in its formative years in America was vintage Marxism. Not only that, but these colonial slackers and society dregs lived among their betters. There was "no separation between the needy and the rest of the community" (Gross). No suburbs, no gated communities, no places to hide from and ignore the huddled masses. Nor were there any "formal institutions," Gross noted, "no poorhouses, hospitals, or asylums in which to control and to segregate the dependent and the deviant."

Over time, as you well know, personalized

charity in the context of the small-scale community changed and "humanitarians abandoned the field to professionals" working for "formal institutions" (Gross). And "with the growth of organized benevolence, people gained an excuse to turn away beggars from their door" by simply directing them to an institution (Gross). Without these "direct, mutual bonds that have the capacity to knit society together, philanthropy, as opposed to charity, sacrificed its moral purpose" (Gross). The breaking of that bond eventually opened the way for charity to be defined in aspirational rather than ameliorative terms, so that the intellectual aspirations of an educational institution or the spiritual aspirations of a religious institution could, and indeed would, take precedence over the more essential and fundamental needs of the poor. The beggars at the door are once again being turned away and are now told to turn to government agencies that are under increasing attack from and demonization by the Ayn Rand austerity crowd led by Paul Ryan and Mitch McConnell. I cannot now think of peace, Patrick, only overthrow.

Michael

The Ever Expanding Universe of Charity

A charity ought to be defined as an institution in which a majority of its clients are vulnerable due to poverty, illness, disability, abuse, neglect, homelessness, hunger, or delinquency.

We have obviously removed ourselves from the kind of personal charity once practiced in America, and by the mid twentieth century, according to Peter D. Hall, in an essay titled "The Welfare State and the Careers of Public and Private Institutions Since 1945," Congress tossed the whole idea of charity down the rabbit hole by creating what we all now know as the 501(c)3 organization for charitable, educational and religious institutions. This new "code," Hall notes, "left the definition of key terms like charitable and philanthropic troublingly vague," thus providing "ample opportunity for expanding the range of activities covered by the term charity." What Hall refers to as "vaguely drawn" IRS provisions might more appropriately be regarded as provisions so broadly drawn that the idea of charity loses any definitive meaning whatsoever and becomes whatever anyone wants it to be. These protean provisions prompted "wealthy individuals, estate planners, and corporations hard-pressed by high taxes to take advantage of every loophole the law allowed" (Hall). "Some business corporations established foundations, donated all their assets to them (reaping generous tax benefits by doing so), then leased back the assets, which they operated as exempt enterprises" (Hall). Not only did these legislative efforts diminish the idea of charity by "enshrining private intentions without regard to public needs" (Hall) but they put charitable giving, with the American Bar Association's Model Nonstock Corporation Statute, "on a businesslike basis" (Bremmer) and encouraged "entrepreneurial management practices and increased commercial activities by charitable corporations" (Hall). This is the corporate face of charity to which people like Pallotta seem totally oblivious.

Sadly, it is a corporatized definition of charity that allows enormously wealthy institutions like the Chautauqua Institution, which I visited last summer, to operate under the aegis of charity. I sat in the Institution's large amphitheater on a sunny summer day in August in a sea of white and gray (wealthy white people with gray hair) listening to a nationally renowned speaker at a lecture event that had to cost in the tens of thousands of dollars, all underwritten by high-priced ticket-holders such as myself and charitable donations to The Chautauqua Foundation. Ah, but think of all that intellectual ferment, that philosophical flowering. What a wonderfully edifying use of that ubiquitous and uniquely American enterprise, the charity. I'm sure the poor, the neglected, the abused, the homeless, the hungry, and the sick, would give up their last soup kitchen meal to be so edified and uplifted.

And, however much I am a critic of the ever expanding universe of charity, I am complicit in the inflationary cosmology of the charitable universe. I am a regular financial contributor now to a local think tank which is known for its intellectual summits and its lectures on topics like the death of Socrates. And yes, it is a charity, so-called, that has demonstrated the capacity to raise millions of dollars. So let me get on the record, Paddy, as to what a charity ought to be in a society that ought to value compassion and a vision of the common good. A charity ought to be defined as an institution in which a majority of its clients are vulnerable due to poverty, illness, disability, abuse, neglect, homelessness, hunger, or delinquency. That obviously means the aspirational (schools) and the spiritual (churches) institutions are out, and hospitals are in.

I'm sure you realize how difficult it is for me, who values the life of the mind more than most, to deny an intellectual institution the status of charity. I did, after all, tell our Cornell Crew colleagues that we're not dinosaurs because we're old; we're dinosaurs because we're intellectually ill-equipped to lead nonprofit institutions dedicated to human development. We are all, I added, various versions of Larry Summers trying to lead Harvard, of the corporati completely out of their depth or, breadth, as the case may be.

Michael

Corporatization's Two Laws

1. Corporation's first law is that the corporation is now the template for all of our nonprofit institutions.
2. Corporatization's second law is the strenuous imitation of corporate culture by nonprofit institutions.

I suppose, Patrick, that not-so-lucky Larry Summers was one of the more meretricious instances of higher education's increasing corporatization—another term, vulgar as it is, that needs defining. Corporatization, in the universe of nonprofits, has at least two laws of physics: the first law is that the corporation, as a result of an originally vague legal definition and nonprofit boards dominated by business people and nonprofit executives stocked from the shelves of the trade schools of business, is now the template for virtually all of our nonprofit institutions. But it isn't just the corporate idea co-opting relatively supine and ill-informed nonprofit leaders. Corporatization's second law is the strenuous imitation of corporate culture by nonprofit institutions. Wherever you look you can see nonprofits enamored with money, marketing and metrics, always eager to tout their business acumen in plans of various kinds—marketing plans, succession plans, and the granddaddy of them all, strategic plans, which, in their formulaic redundancy, are invariably about more marketing, more quality improvement (i.e., standards), and more growth.

One wonders what Mills and Galbraith would have said about the preoccupation of nonprofits with growth. Is growth, or as Mills would have put it, prosperity, the solution to our social ills? The social innovation crowd, again in imitation of business culture, wants to be more entrepreneurial, relying less on established (perhaps moribund) social agencies connected to the status quo, while much of the donor world keeps insisting that there needs to be more collaboration by nonprofits, which they believe will minimize duplication of service and maximize success in ameliorating social problems. They may be right about the idea of collaboration, but they're wrong about who needs to do the collaborating. If the major donors in every community across America were able to collaborate, pool their resources, and apply a Jim Collins-like model for great (not just good) nonprofit institutions, you could virtually eliminate duplication of service and achieve the kind of impact people like Pallotta envision. The problem with collaborating on the donor side of the charitable equation is that the philanthropic practices of the corporate crowd—matching gifts, program funding, funding only capital needs, and a general lack of understanding as to what a great nonprofit (the Collins-like model) ought to be—have contributed to the inefficient use of resources (bloated administrations with armies of fundraisers) by nonprofit institutions. Add to that poisonous practices like Pepsi Fresh, where consumers are encouraged to vote for their favorite charity (with the top vote-getting charity getting a large charitable contribution from Pepsico), and you not only conflate the sale of a not-so-soft soft drink with charitable activity but you degrade the idea of charity (and the idea of voting) by reducing it to a crass commercial enterprise. It's charity degraded down to product pitch. And we all know, of course, that if you bought a coke during your lifetime, you have contributed to another non-charity, education. Perhaps we should quaff a few more cokes, Paddy, but with plenty of rum please.

A More Humanistic Paradigm

Clearly, the corporatized concept of charity and of nonprofit institutions has become the prevailing paradigm.

Patrick, at least my last letter to you ended on a high, with visions of rum, many rums and cokes so as to make our charitable mark on higher (in cost perhaps) education (let's be candid and call it preparation for the business trades) in the land of the soft drink and the home of the consumer as citizen. And that's what I want to talk about today, the civic side of things, not Citizen Kane but Citizen Pepsi Fresh, not visionary big idea entrepreneurial strategic thinking, but rather that thing I'll call the civic soul draggled by coarse corporatism. The corporate class, in freshening up the Pepsi people, has given us the perfect illustration of Marcuse's *One Dimensional Man*, in which "people recognize themselves in their commodities."

This is what Galbraith meant when he argued that our consumer goods economy was geared to the least urgent set of values, what Plato meant by a regime devoted to pleasure rather than virtue and what Tocqueville meant when he observed an unwillingness to participate in assemblies because people were weary from the pursuit of goods. Robert F.

Kennedy, in a speech he gave shortly before he was assassinated in 1968, stated that Americans had come to value the wrong things and had given themselves over to the accumulation of things. A more contemporary take by the political scientist and philosopher Michael Sandel has noted that we have allowed market forces to rewrite the norms that govern social institutions, a development foretold at least a century earlier when Max Weber observed that scientifically and technologically oriented cultures posed threats to social democracies (and by extension social institutions) with their tendency to trash traditional values in favor of efficiency and effectiveness. Thomas Jefferson may have put it better than anyone when he argued that the economic arrangements of a nation would be critical in determining the kind of citizen a society produces. As we enter the second decade of the twenty-first century, I think it's clear that our economic arrangements, which I would characterize as a relentless and wide-ranging corporatization of American culture (the polemicist Chris Hedges believes that we now live in a corporate state hijacked by corporations with ruthless efficiency), have produced not only citizen consumers (Marcuse's commodity) but also institutions, particularly nonprofits, that are little more than a corporate foil.

In its many meager attempts to be

a good corporate citizen, the corporate class continually identifies (though largely misidentifies) causes or agencies to be the recipients of its philanthropic largess, but has never shown much interest, or much knowledge for that matter, of the citizen-building nature of nonprofit institutions. The nonprofit idea, given America's volunteerist democratic beginnings, should have become a major bulwark of democracy. It should have become—to borrow a bit of business jargon—a horizontally integrated social institution that relied on consensus and operated within a constitutional framework of diffused rather than concentrated power. Instead, nonprofits largely have become vertically integrated institutions with power concentrated at the top. This approach to power, as Tocqueville reminds us, is only legitimate when those exercising the power are wise and those over whom it is exercised are ignorant. Those of us who lead social institutions may indeed be ignorant of anything beyond the business bromides by which we operate, but our patrons among the corporate class seem significantly less than wise. Because of their preoccupation with results, they view the value of nonprofits purely in instrumental terms and cannot conceive of a circumstance in which social institutions have intrinsic value. They therefore offer no support of the citizenship-building aspect of institutions that Jefferson envisioned and no encouragement of nonprofits as ends in themselves rather than simply means to ends. Affirming the intrinsic value of charity and the nonprofit institutions that deliver it has nothing at all to do with reimagining a long lost agrarian ideal, but it would require redefining charity as a more disinterested activity and nonprofits as authentic social institutions rather than poor imitations of business. It would require a reimagination of the Jeffersonian ideal that nations should be judged for their "capacity to cultivate in citizens the qualities of character that self-government requires" (Sandel).

Obviously, the paradigm, a term widely used but also widely misunderstood, has changed. The term is misunderstood because its originator, the physicist Thomas Kuhn, defined it in at least twenty different ways in his classic book, *The Structure of Scientific Revolutions.* The book was published fifty years ago to wide acclaim and even wider popularity. Even though some in the halls of the academy regard Kuhn's work as the most important book published in America in the twentieth century, it's not much read anymore and even less understood, except by a few philosophy of science professors in the academy.

Since Kuhn introduced the term "paradigm" in 1962, it has become a central term in our lexicon, particularly our business lexicon. I think what Kuhn meant by it is that the practice of normal everyday science has always been governed by a worldview. The worldview consists of a set of beliefs as to how scientific work should be done, but it also has a set of assumptions that invariably go unquestioned until a new paradigm emerges. A new paradigm generally emerges when the existing one is unable to solve the problems it was set up to solve; thus anomalies occur. So, rather than challenge the assumptions of the existing paradigm, Kuhn argued that normal science routinely reinterpreted conflicting data in ways that would support the paradigm, or it simply ignored conflicting data altogether. Scientific practice, then, made the governing paradigm self-validating, bringing with it a certain theoretical rigidity and a disciplinary dogmatism. Each paradigm creates its own gestalt, its own comprehensive synthesis, so that scientists working within different paradigms with their own prevailing assumptions seem to be living in entirely different worlds.

I think that's why we're living in a nonprofit charitable world very different from the one created, slowly and inevitably since the colonial times and more quickly and comprehensively in the last half century, by the corporate class. The assumptions that govern the new corporate paradigm are all regarded, to borrow Galbraith's term, as conventional wisdom.

They include ideas like charity as a quid pro quo, nonprofits as purely business entities and instrumental results-oriented institutions, an analytical fixation with metrics and data, a governing authority that is titular and concentrated, and a managerial class with a narrow set of business skills. I've tried to chart what the current corporate paradigm looks like compared to a more humanistic one:

Corporate Paradigm	**Humanistic Paradigm**
Charity as quid pro quo	Charity freely given
Nonprofit of instrumental value	Nonprofit as an end in itself
Concentrated power structure	Diffused power structure
Quantitative results	Qualitative results
Clients as means to organizational ends	Clients as ends in themselves
Trained skilled staff (specialists)	Broadly educated staff (generalists)
Brand driven	Driven by client needs
Prescriptive standards	Original principles
Analytical approach	Creative idea development
Constitutional compliance	Constitutional power-sharing
Accountability	Autonomy

Clearly, the corporatized concept of charity and of nonprofit institutions is the prevailing paradigm. No one that I know of has challenged its validity. It's been challenged in broader terms as a corporatization of American culture by intellectuals like Chris Hedges and Morris Berman, and it's been challenged in more particular terms by Diane Ravitch (public education), Gaye Tuchman (higher education) and Michael Sandel (the degradation of democratic norms). Paradoxically, even corporatists like Dan Pallotta have challenged the corporate paradigm of charity by pointing out how ineffective it is, though his solution, to further corporatize an already failing paradigm, is precisely the self-validating practice that Kuhn saw in the realm of normal science.

So where does this put us, Paddy? How did this corporate paradigm come to define charity in general and nonprofits like ours in particular? Is this corporate paradigm really failing in a way that would be obvious to most observers? For Pallotta and others it's failing because it isn't raising enough money and therefore isn't solving major social problems like poverty and AIDS. For them, the paradigm is failing because it isn't sufficiently capitalistic. For me, it's failing because it isn't sufficiently humanistic. What it lacks, in humanistic terms, is noble intent, the intrinsic value of humanity, originality, autonomy, creativity, intellectual curiosity, and a democratic definition of power. The current corporate paradigm, with all its banal buzz words and sanguine marketing slogans, its accountability and compliance, its skill sets and prescriptions, its phony metrics and junk science, its quid pro quo power politics, is so entrenched, so self-validating, so unaware of the humanistic worldview, that our proposal for a senate, for a measure of democratic governance within our own Association, might not, perhaps will not, at next week's conference, prevail. Ciao.

Well, Michael, your last letters certainly make it clear that charity is not what it once was, and nonprofits such as ours, so utterly co-opted by corporate America, are not anything like what they should be, which is, as you effectively argue, democratic institutions. But it may be too early, even with the vote that's supposed to come down in a few days, to go all out with an anti-corporate approach. Too early for all out war with the corporati, with the Steve Davis's of the world. Best to keep your remarks short, eloquent and concentrated on the democratic aspect of the argument.

3

Governance by Commission

If people are not knowledgeable and independent
but instead are a mere mass without any real stake in the
political system, many things might follow,
but government of the people, by the people,
and for the people, will not.
~Alan Ryan

Non-Aggression Pact

Our conundrum is that we have an important
public position which we cannot make public.

Well, Patrick, let me begin with the bad news: there was no vote on the senate proposal, which means the issue festers, or, if you like, ferments, for another year. The good news is that Whitehall actually held, for the first time in at least a decade, a separate International Council Meeting, in its own venue, at a prescribed time, and even sought to establish a quorum for the meeting. And it was the quorum that turned out to be the catch. Steve Davis stepped up to the podium and called the meeting to order and announced that, lacking a quorum, the meeting would have to be adjourned until one could be established at a later time, most likely on-line. A week later, claiming to have established a quorum on their website, in a chat room no less, a motion was made and seconded and approved (not unanimously; we and a few other organizations voted no) to accept the slate of officers and board members for Whitehall. As for the infamous Erie Proposal to establish a senate, it was tabled for review. Review? Review by whom? Really? So what now, my good man, now that we're stuck with this gentlemen's agreement, this non-aggression pact with Eileen Boyer? Our conundrum is that we have an important public position which we cannot make public. Your thoughts?

Michael

Well, if you're going to honor your gentlemen's agreement with Eileen, there's not much you can do except wait to see what they do with this so-called review. But I always thought that Eileen, conflicted as she is by a superego guilt-ridden with ethical concerns, would be different from her Machiavellian predecessors. She has not been so. Why is that? I think it comes down to being a really strong-willed person. Eileen, like most corporate CEO's, is used to getting what she wants when she wants it. And they call this, in the clichéd world of the corporati, a soft skill? But knowing this crowd as I do, having fought the good fight with Eileen's predecessors, my money is on them establishing a task force designed to kill this thing before it has a chance to take hold.

Getting Co-Opted

I simply refuse to be facilitated, handled, marginalized or otherwise co-opted.

Okay, Pennsylvania Soothsayer, Oracle of Bucks County, you were, to borrow one of our regional director's more infelicitous phrases, spot on. Denny McAndrew called me today to ask me to serve on a task force assigned the task of reviewing our current governance structure and process. I thought, until today, that there was only one proposal, our international senate, that one could actually call a governance proposal. But apparently Denny has an alternative proposal in which Eileen has shown some interest. Denny's proposal would separate the role of the international organization. This would give the international organization's board of governors the authority to elect its own board members rather than have that authority, as its currently constituted, rest with the International Council, with, that is, us. The only thing this proposal borrows from ours is the idea of a representative model, with the International Council being made up of one representative from each state association. There would be no senate, no power-sharing, no real democratic process.

I would have agreed to serve on the group if they had had any intention of making it a wide-open discussion involving a few, and only a few, of the principles—three or four of us from the field, three or four of them, including Denny and Eileen—but when Denny explained that this group was going to consist of members of Eileen's International Council Committee, made up of, as you know, local Association board members, and was going to be facilitated by their senior vice-president of training, I gave Denny a firm and final no thank you. I simply refuse to be facilitated, handled, marginalized or otherwise co-opted. Maybe it's time for Gentleman Palermo to be ungentlemanly. Maybe it's time to organize our own meeting somewhere in the middle of the country, Chicago perhaps, and invite any and all Association executives interested in restoring democratic governance to this institution. I'm not in a magnanimous mood, Brother McSweeney. No thoughts of peace today.

Michael

That's the spirit, Palermo; get good and pissed off; keep fighting the good fight. But I have to say that the good fight, no matter what Denny or Eileen does with this goofy group of theirs, should be fought in the International Council. You still have a card to play there. Eventually they'll have to bring your senate proposal to a vote. They're stalling now. They know they've got a broken governance model and they don't know how to fix it. They've already conceded, by actually convening a separate meeting this year with an attempt, however disingenuous, at establishing a quorum, that what they've been doing—two-minute meetings in the context of conference general sessions, no quorum, no credentialed delegates, and most of all, no records—is cavalierly dishonest, unethical, and probably illegal. No formal records of who voted for what? They've got a big problem. Keep up the pressure. Eventually, there has to be a vote up or down on the senate proposal.

The Collectivization Plan

What this plan is really about? Innovation, of course—consistent, efficient, accountable, measurable, systemized and standardized innovation.

Okay, Patrick, how's this for backstory. I talked to Denny and found out that Eileen threatened to fire him. When Denny sent out the notice for the Annual Meeting of the International Council and included the senate proposal on the agenda, he did so without Eileen's approval. When she found out, she walked into his office, not once but several times, and threatened to fire him. Killing colleagues is obviously a corporate skill-set that Eileen lacks. Still, it has made Denny much more cautious about helping our populist revolt prevail. When I pointed out the potential legal ramifications of having no records to support all the constitutional changes they've made in the last decade, he simply said that if and when that legal challenge comes, the records will be there. Maybe the message here is that, if you're not ruthless enough, surround yourself with people who are. Our boy Denny has become one hell of an underboss. His closing comment to me was that Eileen wants to talk to me about something she's working on. A speech perhaps? I thought my speechwriting days with her were over.

It wasn't a speech that Eileen wanted to talk about. It's a paper, a white paper of sorts, thus far untitled, but marked confidential. She sent it to me with one caveat: it's not to be shared with anyone in the field, not yet at least. I intend to honor that injunction, but since you're no longer in the field, as they say, I'd like to summarize it for you and get your opinion on it. It looks like a strategic plan of sorts, with goals, guiding principles, processes, and timelines. Whereas their last strategic plan was driven by growth, this one will be driven by quality.

The paper opens with the idea that our organization is on the threshold of having unparalleled impact on American youth. The foundation of that threshold, she argues, lies in our vision to lift whole generations of children to levels of civic engagement not seen since the founding of our nation, and in the size and scale of our institution that now has 5,000 local organizations and 300,000 volunteer, board, and professional leaders. Eileen's strategic planning guru, our old friend David Stewart, has referred to this dubious achievement (I say dubious because some of the growth numbers are real but much of it, as you know, is pure prestidigitation) as having arrived at a point of critical mass. Implicit in her opening paragraph is the idea that God is good, God is great, but growth is, in the corporati created universe, greater still.

But to realize this newfound potential, she goes on to say, we need to come together in new ways so as to deliver even higher quality services that achieve measurable outcomes and solution-level impact. We need to cease being an organization of organizations and become a system of interdependent organizations. This, somehow, would make us more relevant, more current, more nimble? It would enable us to more fully capitalize on our collective size and the strength of our brand. It would enable us to more effectively compete for resources and, following the Pallotta Principle, have the greatest possible impact.

Paddy, we're just getting started here, but you should, nevertheless, have the warm fuzzies by now, so here's a little doggerel ditty for you:

Let's be nimble
Let's be quick
No need to jump
Over a candlestick
Like a laser beam
We can achieve the dream
To capitalize
On our collective size.

Stay with me now. It gets better.

To become this high impact, interdependent system, we must collectively (there's that word again) establish principles, structures and operating practices that bind us together with clearly articulated outcomes; deliver evidence-based programs with measurable outcomes (the scientific revolution marches on); increase consistency and collective (yes, indeed) accountability; foster alignments and shared arrangements to create the necessary infrastructure to deliver high impact; and finally (well, not really), establish structures and processes that increase dialogue and opportunities for meaningful input into the direction, goals and actions that drive the Movement. Yep, I can see it now, lot's of structured, collective, accountable, interdependent, high impact, evidence-based... dialogue? That's right, dialogue. Well, not yet. There are still more collective goodies.

If we do all of this collectivizing, and thus strengthen the Movement as an interdependent system, we will be able to make a measurable difference, apply more resources to mission, achieve peak efficiency through shared services, ensure consistency and high operating standards, and attract and compete for new resources needed to increase impact and generate growth.

And I'm still on page one of a five-page opus.

Page one concludes with a poetic flourish called The Bottom Line. You get a chart of sorts, let's call it a matrix (one of David Stewart's pet terms), with a bullet box on the left that's titled, Bottom Line: What This **IS** About, and a bullet box on the right that's titled, Bottom Line: What This Is **NOT** About.

What this paper (and plan) supposedly **IS** about is...

- Clustering resources
  to create efficiencies
- Achieving consistency
  to increase impact
- Providing more opportunities for
  (I'm not kidding) innovation

What it's supposedly **NOT** about is...

- Creating company owned stores

- Imposing and enforcing a set of rules
- Forcing mergers
- Creating bureaucracy
- Making every local organization look alike

I'm thinking that this is a version of the Heisenberg Uncertainty Principle, which really has to do with the little stuff in the quantum world, writ large. The principle, according to the physicist Brian Greene, essentially says that reality has a dual nature to it. So "you can measure precisely how fast an electron is moving, but in doing so you will contaminate your ability to determine with precision its position." The duality here is that when you look at what the bottom line **IS** is doing, its plan, its activity, its movement, you lose your ability to see that it has been replaced by what the bottom line is **NOT**. I'm going to call this The Eileen Boyer Uncertainty Planning Principle.

I had senior staff look at this paper. One of the tasks was to identify key terms. We called it a Literary Analysis of the Bottom Line. Or What Is Not, Is, And What Is, Is Not. What it is, is this: consistency, efficiency, accountability, and collectivity; standards, practices, processes, and analyses; outcomes, measures, structures, and resources; inputs, outputs, impacts; systematize and capitalize—none of which, we are told, will lead to bureaucracy, to more standards and rules, to more mergers, to the creation of company owned stores. What this plan is really about? Innovation, of course—consistent, efficient, accountable, measurable, systematized and standardized, innovation. It would take a miracle of biblical proportions to systematize and standardize our way to innovation.

I'd go on with further exegesis of the new Boyer bible, but I think that that's enough data analysis for one collectivized, interdependent, innovative, entrepreneurial day. The big development recently is that Denny McAndrew believes a sit-down between me and Eileen has the potential to resolve this whole governance crisis. Looks like our Sancho Panza from the hallowed halls of Whitehall is suddenly seeing windmills. But Denny said he could arrange the sit-down, and I agreed. Eileen, who will be in New York a few weeks from now to meet with some corporate mogul, agreed to have dinner with me there. It'll have to be dinner and drinks, or make that drinks and dinner, or maybe just drinks.

Michael

I can only say that this new approach is tactically brilliant. What I assume is happening—you would know better than I—is that their latest attempt to standardize and franchise the institution is not working as Eileen had hoped it would. The fear-mongering approach of supposedly protecting the brand from scandal just isn't working. It's too negative. But wrapping yourself in the positive promise of having greater impact in the lives of these kids, that is convincing, compelling, brilliant. It's like the tyrant touting equality, or the corporate titan, the all-powerful CEO, touting the freedom inherent in free enterprise. She might as well have wrapped herself in the American flag. Impact, to borrow a trope from the corporate crowd, is an easy sell. Democratic process is not. Good luck.

Seeking Equanimity

These were the things I found in life,
the things I came to value.

Well, Patrick, one bourbon into our dinner meeting, at a cozy but boisterous Italian restaurant in the West Village, things were going quite well. We exchanged a few family pleasantries, stories about adult children and grandchildren, and reminiscences from the old days when we worked together and Whitehall was still headquartered in New York. Eileen's seemingly impenetrable wall of reserve, which we have all witnessed over the years, came down momentarily as we confided in each other about the future of our families, about our prospects for retirement, about life and human happiness in general. I certainly noticed, and I assume someone as perceptive as Eileen noticed, how different our lives were weighted on the happiness scale. With work the prevailing preoccupation of her life, her talk of a burgeoning family life—her son and daughter-in-law and granddaughter are now living nearby—seemed to have a sentimental tone of time lost. This was a reminder to me that in the early years of our friendship, when I was still working for her in the big house, I mentioned on a few occasions the importance of having some balance in life between the personal and the professional. But I stopped saying this to her when it became apparent that she didn't want to hear it anymore. The happiness talk also reminded me that in those early years she would comment on how hard I worked, as if this were a compliment about which I would be pleased. I was not at all pleased. I was then and remain today more interested in the creative side of work and life, in the idiosyncratic, in intellectual curiosity in general. Looking back on it now, it occurs to me that she was really talking about herself. And what I said to her that night about my own travels and travails on the path to the good life brought me back to the balance, the equilibrium, the equanimity I sought as a young man. I never quite achieved it. My seeking it has probably been too serendipitous and undisciplined ever to do so. But what I came to value as the good life was simple, true and timeless: love, friendship, meaningful work, and what Allan Bloom called the theoretical life, the life of the mind. These were the things I found in life, the things I came to value.

Tyro to Tutor

She took umbrage with the suddenly expansive tutorial tone I was taking with her.

By the time dinner arrived, and a second bourbon had come and gone, I was in an expansive mood. I don't need to tell you that Eileen is a penetrating listener but not a patient one. You can talk to her, but not expansively. It was as if, for this one occasion at least, our roles had reversed. Whereas I had always been the loyal lieutenant, the tyro to her tutor, listening to her advice and direction, I had the palpable impression, perhaps due to the time I had given to the topics we were discussing, perhaps due in some small way to the breadth of reading and reflecting and writing I had done over the years, that I had seemingly and suddenly, for this one night at least, become the tutor to her tyro. I had the vivid but uneasy impression that my old superior, my old friend and colleague sitting across from me, had in some way been diminished by her own success, that devoting herself to a corporate climb characterized by corporate values and intellectual philistinism, and making the narrow confines of work her whole life, made who and what she was to become in the three decades that I had known her someone smaller personally and less able intellectually than she otherwise would have been.

I was reminded of something she said to me after we had been working together for a while and she trusted me enough to confide to me that one of our senior vice-presidents, who was then her direct boss, now had nothing new to teach her. That is exactly what I felt that night in New York, that in the narrowly prescribed path she had taken, one in which the wider paths of love and friendship and broad intellectual curiosity had been left largely unexplored, there was now nothing new—save the finer points of fundraising—that Eileen could teach me. Her increasingly glacial look and clipped tone and her relatively weak arguments (weak for her, for someone who always took pride in her ability to make logically incisive arguments) were all indications to me that she took umbrage with the suddenly expansive tutorial tone I was taking with her. She seemed, in a word, shaken—by my confidence, by my passion, by my utter temerity.

An Exercise in Power, not Democracy

Power over people is only legitimate when those exercising that power are enlightened and those over whom it is exercised are ignorant.
~Tocqueville

Our discussion was pretty wide-ranging, with me doing most of the ranging, but we began with the topic that Eileen believed our meeting was purportedly about, namely her new paper, her new plan to use the idea of impact to complete the ongoing corporatization of the institution. She conceded that the governance issue was important, but that the reorganization her new impact plan called for was a more important priority. Her impact plan, she argued, to be worked out by a new commission that would presumably engage the entire field in the re-evaluation process, needed to come first, though she did agree that some work could be done on our governance model while the commission did its work.

I tried, at first, to be diplomatic. I tried to point out how encouraged I was that she thought our governance model needed to be reformed.

Not necessarily reformed, she said, but reviewed and, if possible, improved. She added that a representative model had some promise.

I said, "Don't you think we need to work out how our decision-making entity, the International Council, is structured before we start making changes to the structure of the organization?"

"No, these are strategic planning issues."

Ah yes, I thought, that good old corporate cooking called strategic planning. "This is much more than a planning issue," I said. "Since this new commission is explicitly about changing the nature of the relationship between the local organizations and the international organization, from an organization of organizations to a system of interdependent organizations, from one of expanded local autonomy to one of limited local autonomy, it is a constitutional issue that needs to be resolved by the governance entity in place for that purpose, the International Council. That means, quite simply, that our governance model, which many of us believe is broken, needs to be fixed first. And it needs to be fixed—discussed and debated and decided—in the only venue appropriate for that purpose, the International Council. This impact plan is going to launch the third commission process in less than five years, which is having the unintended but unfortunate effect of undermining the democratic nature of this institution. The Council is the only entity through which we can or should change our constitution and therefore our institution."

The pleasant half-smile Eileen mustered for preliminaries dropped down to dour. She insisted that the plan she was promoting would not diminish local autonomy, nor would the commission process be undemocratic. The commission would in fact "reach out to the entire field, engaging in real-time input, feedback, advice and counsel."

I quickly countered that if this commission was anything like the ones that preceded it, the whole process will be nothing more than an exercise in controlled political speech.

"That's ridiculous," she said.

"Characterizing highly scripted focus groups as town hall meetings," I said," is positively Orwellian."

"You're being hyperbolic," she said.

"We're told we can't ask our own questions, but instead have to answer the scripted questions that your staff facilitators are directed to ask us, and you want to characterize this as advice and counsel from the field? That's an exercise in power, not democracy. As Tocqueville aptly put it, power over people is only legitimate when those exercising that power are enlightened and those over whom it is exercised are ignorant. We, in the field, are hardly ignorant."

In her iciest tone, Eileen said that I was full of Tocqueville quotes. I took the subtext to mean that I'm also full of shit. She then added: "Does that mean I'm enlightened?"

"Not when you bypass our constitution and govern the organization by one commission after another. Constitutions are supposed to be statements of general principles, not compliance documents. They're supposed to be a protection against the concentration of power, not instruments of regulation, of concentrated power."

"Give me one concrete example of this supposed concentration of power," she said. "We've put requirements in place for things like criminal and child abuse checks. How is that concentrating power?"

"That's fine," I said, "but making the Standards of Organizational Effectiveness, all two hundred and fifty or so of them, a requirement of membership is a ridiculously long and prescriptive thing to attach to our constitution. It should be used as a resource for organizational planning and nothing more. It's analytic overkill. It'll have the deleterious effect of bureaucratizing every aspect of the organization, turning us into a cookie-cutter, paint-by-the-numbers institution. And as much as I like and respect our regional service director (our old friend Doug Hays), I don't have any desire to have him come in as if he were some kind of auditor sitting down with my board members evaluating us against these so-called Standards. It gives the international organization a management arm into my organization that neither I nor my board wants."

By now the look on Eileen's face was positively glacial.

Her hesitation encouraged me to continue. "We're in the thrall of a corporate culture that is re-defining us," I said. "We shouldn't acquiesce to the corporate culture. We shouldn't let them define us in narrow business terms. We should instead make an affirmative defense of who and what we are, and if we did that, I think they could still be persuaded to support us—but on our terms, not theirs. They, whether we want to acknowledge it or not, need us."

The temperature between us underwent a sudden transformation, from white ice to crimson lava. Glowering now, Eileen repeated, in a voice loud enough for those seated near us to hear, "You're hyperbolicl!"

"And why do this now", I went on, "when you've got a succession plan in place."

"What succession plan?" she said in a raised voice.

"The one that's positioned two senior vice presidents to succeed you. The one that looks a lot like the succession plans that the international organization has somehow required us local organizations to have."

"There is no succession plan."

"Eileen, everybody in the field knows about this. Everybody's talking about it, speculating about it. This is what imitating the corporate world gets you."

That final corporate comment, implying, as it did, that she was some kind of corporate foil, would be my last and most hurtful hyperbolic punch. There followed a few shouts measure for measure, after which she stoically paid the bill and we walked out of the restaurant together to go our separate ways.

It's obvious that I will never write another speech for Eileen Boyer, nor could I, even if she asked. But the more important matter is whether our friendship, which has lasted three decades, has been irreparably damaged. Regrettably, Paddy, I think that it has.

Eileen's just not used to being challenged like that, Michael. This isn't a small mom and pop operation she's running; it's a fairly good-sized corporation, over which, she, as the CEO (it's worth noting that the title used to be International Director), is in complete command. Other than Denny McAndrew, whom she has threatened to fire on several occasions, she's surrounded by people who by inclination are sycophantic or who have just given up trying to persuade someone as stubborn as Eileen.

On the friendship front, I think that over time she'll come around. She has a good heart and she genuinely values your friendship and—your "hyperbolic" nature aside—your intellect. But her refusal to see the cogency of your argument, namely that the direction of the institution should be decided democratically by a senate in which a true majority is the ultimate decider of things, tells me that your senate idea will end up in the junk-heap of our institution's history. As bad as that honest estimate sounds, I still believe you have to, as any good contrarian has to do, keep fighting the fight. You have to, as they say, call the question.

The Democratic Patina

Dialogue on a plan that's already been planned

Well, Patrick, a question has been called, but it's not whether we need a senate to reestablish the institution's democratic bona fides; it's whether Whitehall can exploit the idea of impact to complete the transformation of the institution into what Eileen has described as "an interdependent system" sufficiently standardized "to capitalize on our collective size." She has, as she stubbornly said she would, gone public with her paper just one week prior to the conference and the Council meeting.

In an email memorandum to the field, written in the elevated rhetoric of a major speech, she launched the new initiative, Leveraging for Impact, attaching to it a distilled down version of the five-page paper I described to you in a previous letter. Referring to us, as she often does, as a Movement, she argued that we were a great American success story, not because we were forced to change but because of the vision and engagement of the Movement and our collective commitment to its destiny.

She then referred to her new front group, the Commission for the Second Century, falsely attributing to it the new vision (which isn't new at all) that success ought to be in the reach of every child and whole generations of children ought to be lifted to a level of civic engagement not seen since the founding of our nation, a vision that actually got articulated in a speech that I wrote for her a couple of years ago. This vision, she wrote—invoking one of her favorite phrases—calls on us to be as deep in our impact as we are broad in our reach. What broad in our reach means is that Whitehall's not going to neglect the most iconic of corporate bromides—growth. Like publish or perish, it's grow or die. But now she wants to add to that an equally concerted effort on the quality side of the corporate planning equation. At relatively modest levels, growth and quality can converge, but at a certain level they do indeed diverge, with either too much growth compromising quality or too great an emphasis on quality diminishing growth. The enormous growth in the number of kids served over the last decade, for example, has not been matched by a commensurate growth in the number of staff working directly with the kids (staff growth has largely been in managerial jobs like fundraising and marketing), thus attenuating both staff to kid ratios and the overall quality of service. But Whitehall would never admit that quality has been compromised by growth. Rather, Eileen, with CEO-like hubris, expects to do both at the highest levels, so that every kid we encounter is expected to go to college and to succeed in material terms. Maybe, to be fair, her somewhat naïve notion about the destinies of children is simply more romantic than arrogant, more hopeful than realistic.

From there she went back to the broad theme of modern America where the economic, political and social realities have dramatically changed. How so, she doesn't specifically say. What she does say is that this change, this new environment, makes our vision more relevant and more challenging. And one must, in this new economic reality, have a challenge. Without a challenge, there is no narrative; without a narrative, no plan, no growth, no quality. And what does this new environment calls on us to do? To work in new and interconnected ways. It calls on us to demonstrate deeper impact with even more measurable results. It calls on us to capitalize on our interdependence while preserving our independence. It calls on us to be more efficient, more effective in our ways of work. It calls on us to be what most American institutions must now be, corporate clichés, with vertically integrated, anti-democratic power structures (otherwise known as interdependent) efficiently capitalizing on bottom-line measurable results.

Given these new realities and the voices of board and professional leaders heard in focus groups across America (one has to salute her candor in characterizing as focus groups what her staff have repeatedly referred to as town hall meetings), Eileen introduced us to her new initiative, Leveraging for Impact, and its accompanying briefing paper, Organizing for Impact, to which she encouraged us to give thoughtful consideration, so that, as a Movement (What Movement? Whitehall is the Movement.), we can deepen our impact, advance our vision, raise new resources and assure our relevance in a new world. Another new world order.

Her paper, now titled, is shorter (only two pages), with a three-paragraph introduction that mentions kids and the importance of safe places to go and great mentors to guide them, noting that 1.2 million kids drop out of school each year. The rest of the paper, other than positing a new emphasis on academic success, had the same false note of her original. The objective, she wrote, is not to shift to company-owned stores, build greater bureaucracy, or make all local organizations look alike. Rather, the Commission is charged with proposing recommendations to capitalize on our collective size and potential as an interdependent system, and in doing so, leverage our collective size and strength to achieve greater impact with evidence-based, measurable outcomes.

Eileen closed her letter by announcing that Whitehall, along with her Commission group and training staff, will conduct round-table discussions with local executives at next week's international conference, to, as she says, launch (she rather likes launching and capitalizing) this critical dialogue (on a plan that's already done? a dialogue?) which will continue over the months ahead for local input (nice technocratic term) at various forums (translation: highly scripted focus groups) across the Movement.

Paddy, it positively warms the cockles of my heart to know that we're going to be engaging in all this dialogue so as to give a democratic patina to a plan that's already been planned.

Ciao Ciao,
Michael

A Melancholy Spectacle

It is naively utopian to believe that the masses will rise up to claim their legitimate right to govern.

Dear Patrick, with another international conference having fallen off the event horizon, it seems I have fallen off with it and now find myself in a black hole of despondency. Before that International Council Meeting was called to order in the early morning of the last full day of the conference, I was able to catch up with Denny McAndrew in conference headquarters who explained to me in a hasty and hushed conversation that the Council Meeting would occur in the context of the round-table discussions of Eileen's Leveraging for Impact plan. He assured me there would be a microphone in the room and I would get an opportunity to speak from the floor, but I would be limited to two minutes. So I took the roughly ten minutes of remarks that I had planned to make and revised them down to two. I realized afterwards that Denny—whether intentionally or unintentionally, I do not know—misled me, and I could have, and indeed should have, delivered the ten-minute Demosthenean philippic that I had originally planned.

When I walked through one of the ballroom entrances where the Council Meeting was to take place, I expected to enter a smaller sectioned-off room with a hundred or so delegates in attendance. Instead, I was stunned to find the entire ballroom filled with delegates seated at round tables, probably about fifteen hundred or so, all of them undoubtedly eager to declare their fealty for the new commission plan to the international staffer assigned to facilitate at their table. At the other end of this mammoth room, seated on a raised platform, was the metaphorical elephant in the room: the reserved, almost stoic Eileen Boyer; the genial but still slightly manic facilitator genius, David Stewart; the new chairman of the international board, Edward Holbrook, a very tall and solemn man, languid but dignified, a corporate CEO well-known for his historic brand-building; and our man Denny McAndrew, who was standing in for the board secretary to take the minutes of the about-to-be-convened International Council Meeting. As Denny promised, there was a single standing microphone not far from the mammoths on stage but virtually invisible to the focus group subjects, mostly executive directors but some board volunteers too, who were seated in rounds of ten. I found a seat at a table right next to this lonely loudspeaker that no one in this great hall but me would use and waited for his majesty, Not So Fast Eddie Holbrook, to calmly and deliberatively call the Council Meeting to order.

There was, of course, no real Council Meeting; we were all there, quite obviously, for the real event, the focus group follies, which, a la Ziegfeld, would turn out to be all schtick and no substance. Softly, genially, Holbrook announced that The Erie Proposal was now under review by a task group (Denny's group, which I declined to join so as not to be facilitated into submission as these supine souls were about to be facilitated) and would be brought back for consideration at a later date. Before adjourning this two-minute tour de force, Holbrook asked if anyone would like to comment, at which point I stood up, turned to face the microphone standing next to me, and introduced myself. I must not have gotten close enough to the microphone, because, by the time I finished my brief introduction, Denny had already scurried off the stage and was standing in front of me adjusting the microphone so I could be properly heard. This was a rather risky gesture on Denny's part, a kind of public declaration of where his loyalties lay. Even though he had advised me to limit my comments to two minutes, he undoubtedly wanted me to be heard. Eileen and Holbrook, I'm quite sure, would have preferred no comment at all, especially from me.

So, however brief it was to be, I now had my moment, with an audience much larger than I could have imagined, and this is what I said:

"For those of you who are relatively new to the field, the International Council of today is not anything like it once was. There was, not that many years ago, a long-standing tradition of being able to speak from the floor at Council meetings. The recent practice, over the last decade or so, of having no one speak, is an aberration, an unhealthy, anti-democratic aberration. The point is: you've got a right to speak here. If you've got something to say, I implore you, stand up and say it.

"I do have something to say, and I don't want to be shunted off to some focus group to say it. The Erie Proposal, which Mr. Holbrook perfunctorily referenced, has now been brought up at two Council meetings in two years, and the fact remains that it still has not gotten a fair hearing before a national audience like this nor has it gotten a vote up or down. The two minutes or so that I have been allotted here today will hardly suffice as a fair hearing. I'd need at least forty-five minutes just to present it, not counting the time necessary for debate and discussion. We think that our international organization, at a minimum, has a legal and an ethical obligation to allow The Erie Proposal, which would establish an International Senate, *in addition to,* the International Council, to come to a vote at next year's International Council Meeting—and in a minute I'm going to make a motion to that effect.

"I have been told, by Eileen herself, and here today by Mr. Holbrook, that although the governance issues raised by our proposal are important, they're not as important as the work of this new commission, which, they seem to believe, needs to proceed first, needs to have the priority.

"But we in Pennsylvania believe that two

years is too long. We have begun to believe that the International Association has no real intention of giving this proposal a fair hearing and a vote up or down. That belief has led us to consider other courses of action in the last year.

"It was suggested that we convene our own national gathering to debate and discuss The Erie Proposal. We rejected that.

"It was suggested that we go over Eileen's head directly to the international board. We rejected that.

"It was suggested that we use the internet and every other available resource to politic our position to the field. We rejected that.

"Long before the Leverage for Impact paper went out to the field, I was given a draft of this paper, by Eileen, who asked me to keep it confidential. And I did.

"At every turn, we, the advocates for a democratic form of governance for our Movement, have acted fairly, and honorably. Our international organization, sadly, has not.

"Their last commission process tried to use the threat of scandal to drive standardization and centralization. This latest commission is taking a more positive approach, the idea of achieving greater impact, to drive the same agenda.

"If you look at the paper they just sent out, the one at your place right now, and a survey they sent out a few weeks ago, you will see that certain themes keep recurring. These include centralizing and standardizing, consistency and efficiency, accountability and measurability—all within the context of an interdependent structure.

"The survey they sent out noted that this commission and the paper that inspired it would transform us from a network of local organizations to a consistent system of organizations. Interdependent structure, consistent system, these are not the words you would use, the ideas you would invoke, if you were truly interested in a transformational vision of the future. This is a vision all right, of a top-down, vertically-integrated corporation, not of a community-based social institution like the Youth Association International.

"The fundamental point I want to make about governance is that the use of commissions—this is our third in five years—is eroding the constitutional role and authority and effectiveness of the International Council, and in the process is degrading the democratic norms of this institution. Here, in the International Council, is where our constitution says we should consider transformational change.

"Before I make my motion, I would simply say that I have decided not to participate in the focus group session to follow, because to do so would make me complicit in our international organization's attempt to deny us the national stage, the senate that is the centerpiece of our proposal, on which we as a Movement could democratically discuss and debate any changes to our constitution, however transformational they might be. To do so would be to admit that there are no longer any legitimate delegates to a real Council under the aegis of a real constitution, but only focus group subjects whose real fealty is to a standardized, centralized corporation.

"So, here is my motion: that The Erie Proposal be placed back on the agenda for the 2011 International Council Meeting and be brought to the floor for discussion, debate, and a vote.

The silence that followed seemed to have the depth of deep space, of a place devoid of anything but dark matter. No one else came forward to speak. No one seconded my motion. I thought that perhaps one of our Cornell Crew colleagues would at least second the motion, but no one came forward. I was, in the words of George Will, in that soundless solitary moment, the melancholy spectacle of the populist leader, the supposed man of the people, to whom the people were utterly indifferent.

But Holbrook, more of a gentleman than I, surprised me by announcing that our proposal, along with the recommendations of the commission, would be on the agenda for the

2011 International Council Meeting.

So, Paddy, that is how things now stand. A year seems like a long time to wait, but at least we will have our day, we will have our vote, we will have this one last chance to recapture the democratic spirit of this venerable, century-old institution. Though I cannot say I'm sanguine about the possibility of prevailing, Paddy. The concurrence of letting this political illegitimacy languish for so long with such an incurious and corporatized cast of characters makes me think it is naively utopian to believe that the masses will rise up to claim their legitimate right to govern.

Your melancholy Michael

You know, it is obvious to me, looking at all of this political wrangling from a distance, looking at it from the modest perch of retirement, that you are simply speaking truth to power, Palermo. That's pretty good stuff in and of itself. You make your old mentor proud, but I don't need to tell you that you've got a long way to go, another whole year to rally the troops. But I still say we're gonna win, Palermo; we're gonna win.

By the by, I picked up the book that you recommended for our Cornell Crew Meeting, which I'm giving a thorough reading. That's the least I can do since the rest of the Crew will probably do nothing more than read an on-line account of this guy Canada and his Harlem Children's Zone. This guy is a real operator.

4

The Privatization of Public Education

The things of greatest value are precisely those things that cannot be measured, and if we cannot measure what is valuable, we will come to value what is measurable.
~Robert Birnbaum

Geoffrey Canada Regime

There is no attending to the civic identities of children in Canada's educational regime, nor is there any attending to the affective dimensions of a child's life.

Reading, whether it is a book about contemporary educational reform or a more classical look at education like Plato's Republic, is in itself insufficient if one's aspiration is to live—in a realm big or small—a life of the mind. My own intellectual realm, though small and insignificant, has at least left me with the understanding that one has to add thought, sometimes considerable thought and reflection, to venture out of Plato's cave into the light, into the essence of things, into a deeper understanding.

I thought that's what Patrick McSweeney had done when our last Cornell Crew Meeting was convened high above Manhattan in the big building with the most telling of American names, The Empire State Building. I thought this because, as he sat down at the conference table with his trademark professorial slouch, with his baggy tweed coat and his food-stained tie and rumpled white shirt, I saw that he had, as promised, read the book we were to talk about as part of our agenda, a book about the Harlem-based education reformer and darling of the corporate class, Geoffrey Canada. I also saw that Patrick's paperback copy of the book was pretty well worn, almost tattered, as if it had been not so much read as chewed on and mulled over and generally picked apart. The multitude of post-it notes popping out of its pages gave the book a disheveled look much like the shabby eminence of its reader, all stained and rumpled and disarrayed, but in its way, still stately.

So when it came time to talk about the book, I turned to Patrick and asked him to open the discussion with any observations he'd like to make. When he began to talk about making investments in young people and other topics he had regaled us with at other meetings on other days in other years, I cut him off dismissively and started to make my own observations about the book. Patrick later told me that he'd forgotten his reading glasses and couldn't read the copious notes he had stuck onto the pages of the book. I didn't realize until later that day, until Patrick's wife Mary Margaret explained it to me, that Patrick sometimes got disoriented in the present, but if you talked to him about the past, his mental acuity was much sharper. With that disheartening lesson learned, I never cut Patrick off again but instead looked for opportunities for him to talk about the time that still mattered to him, the time that he could still eloquently invoke, the past. The stoic and sage Seneca, who thought the present short, the future doubtful, and the past certain, would most certainly have agreed.

After unkindly and regrettably dismissing my old mentor, I started telling my Cornell Crew colleagues what I'd learned from reading my more pristine copy of Paul Tough's book, *Whatever It Takes*, about the widely acclaimed Harlem Children's Zone and its even more famous founder, Geoffrey Canada. Not surprisingly, no one other than Patrick and I had read Tough's book, but everyone at the table—ten of us in all—had heard about and read accounts of Canada and his purportedly innovative approach to educating inner-city children living in poverty. They all knew, for instance, that Canada had staked out a ninety-seven block Zone of Harlem, which the president of the United States praised as an "all-encompassing, all-hands-on-deck antipoverty effort" with services for children and adults that could only be characterized as comprehensive: from Baby College for the parents, who could, after acquiring the knowledge and parenting skills required, start positively affecting the development of their children, especially cognitive development, beginning at birth, to his Promise Academy Charter Schools which were based on what Tough described as a ruthlessly capitalistic business model, an educational model that meant longer school hours for kids and teacher accountability for students' standardized test scores.

I knew I would not have long with my Cornell Crew colleagues, who tended to be impatient with ideas, especially ideas from books that did not seem immediately relevant to the running of their own institutions. But Paul Tough's book, it was clear to me, is eminently relevant to the question of where we, the Youth Association International, are headed as an institution and as a nation in envisioning a future for our children. We are headed—and one can see it in the educational metrics implicit in Eileen Boyer's impact plan—toward a change in mission from guidance and youth development to becoming a an educational institution.

As for Geoffrey Canada, aside from his

cultural vision of transforming a Harlem neighborhood, a Zone, as he calls it, into a middle class model "focused on success, learning, working hard, and getting to college" (Tough), which one could argue is more laudable than the alternative of removing kids from their neighborhood and putting them into boarding schools, Canada has nothing educationally innovative to offer. In fact, he and his billionaire board president, the Wall Street hedge-fund manger Stanley Drunkenmiller, offer little more than a Puritanical paean to hard work and to every business bromide in this billionaire's book. The vision, writes Tough, that formed in Canada's mind was of "an alternative to the traditional social service agency: something bigger and more efficiently run, an organization that would bypass the sentimental (appeals to donors) and instead offer, in exchange for substantial financial commitment, results—measurable, quantifiable outcomes that even the coldest-hearted capitalist would appreciate." This was a perfect complement to Drunkenmiller, whom Tough described as a small government Republican who believed in the wisdom of markets, and who also believed that "the tools of corporate America—management consultants, long-range plans, marketing data, quarterly targets—had created the strongest economy in the history of the world, but in the charitable sector, those tools were being ignored in favor of guesswork and good intentions."

Nothing like a straw man in the hands of a bully billionaire. Though they have little or no scientific legitimacy, quantifiable outcomes were standard in the nonprofit world long before Canada and Drunkenmiller came onto the national scene. The nonprofit world is nothing like the sentimental sob sister that Drunkenmiller characterizes it as; it has, instead, been relentlessly corporatized over the past few decades. Virtually every nonprofit operating today is a business enterprise, driven by the very corporate tools—strategic plans, marketing plans, and plenty of data—that Drunkenmiller wrongly contends are ignored. What is actually being ignored in education today are reforms of a distinctly educational nature, as opposed to those that offer little more than privatization of the public school, that address little more than the political and economic arrangements surrounding public education. What is being ignored, by Canada and Drunkenmiller and many others, who seem to have no ideas outside the realm of business and Calvinist ideology, are truly innovative educational ideas and approaches.

Some of the things Canada is doing—his comprehensive approach to ameliorating poverty in the inner city, his idea of working with kids from birth to college completion—are clearly admirable. The paradox surrounding this charismatic figure—one who, by the way, probably would not have made it to Bowdoin College under a regime in which standardized tests determined your educational destiny—is that his approach and philosophy are comprehensive culturally but narrow educationally. Canada's philosophy begins with an unabashed embrace of corporate culture's emphasis on (supposedly) quantifiable results, educational achievement narrowly defined by standardized test scores, the discipline and hard work embodied in a much longer and very likely exhausting Dickensian school day, early intervention, racial pride, and cognitive development culminating in a college education.

What is missing, aside from anything innovative educationally, is, to borrow a phrase from the political philosopher Michael Sandel, any kind of formative ideal. There is, for example, no attending to the civic identities of children in Canada's educational regime, nor is there any attending to the affective dimensions of a child's life. Children in this regime are largely solitary beings requiring cognitive development rather than social beings requiring deep human connection. The ability of children to make their way in the world then is cognitive not psychological, and it is not dependent on the strength of personal attributes other than the narrow emphasis on hard work. Human happiness is implicitly defined as educational accomplishment ultimately measured by college completion, a job, a home, and other middle class goods.

The good life then is one in which kids grow up to have more of life's goods. For a thinker like Aristotle, having more of life's goods at least meets one of the pre-conditions, but not the most important one, of a good life. A good life needs much more to fill it out than material goods and aspirations; it needs a formative ideal that cannot be adequately nurtured by educational philistines; it needs a public education regime that sees the intrinsic value of children and "finds a way to cultivate in citizens a concern for the whole, a dedication to the common good" (Sandel). For philosophical thinkers like Michael Sandel, the public school is a site of civic education, a place where "justice is not only about the right way to distribute things; it's about the right way to value things" (Sandel).

The *Atlantic* writer Ta-Nehisi Coates, writing about the kind of school he wanted for his son Samori, wrote this about the values that ought to be inherent in a child's education: "I don't actually want Samori in a school that's preparing him for college…I want him in a school that's preparing him to question the world, that nurtures his formidable curiosity…I hope he learns to be passionate about something. If he grew up to be a curious, humble, reflective dude who was passionate about operating a fork-lift, the boy would be all right with me."

Geoffrey Canada's world, by allowing, as Sandel would describe it, the market to rewrite the norms that govern a social institution like the public school, would be an inhospitable place for a kid like Samori. Even within his own organization, Canada had at least one of his staff, his middle school principal, Terri Grey, telling him that his relentless business model was much too narrow an approach to educating children. Grey was a proponent of a more holistic model, one that was "as much about making emotional connections as it was about drilling a kid with information" (Tough). Grey wanted to educate the whole child and avoid the burnout that she thought would inevitably come, for kids and teachers, as a result of Canada's results-oriented, test-prep approach (Tough). What Grey saw unfolding in Canada's test-prep paradigm, with its unrelenting cramming and preparing for standardized tests, was a de-emphasis on classes like music and gym which "Grey thought were essential to creating well-rounded students who could succeed not just at multiple-choice tests, but in life" (Tough). What Grey and others like Kate Shoemaker, the Harlem Children's Zone's director of policy and special projects, saw, and a corporatist like Canada could not countenance, was that "on top of the hours of cognitive training, what made the difference in many students' lives was a personal connection that was impossible to measure..." (Tough). So for me, Terri Grey, whom Canada ultimately fired, is the hero of the story that Tough tells in *Whatever It Takes*, because she had the courage and the wisdom to fight for a conception of the good life, to fight for the idea that it takes a whole child, a well-rounded human being, one with the curiosity and passion of a Samori Coates, to succeed in life.

But my business-friendly colleagues on my Cornell Crew looked at this whole matter of education reform and how we as a nonprofit youth development institution ought to respond to it through the corporate lens of Stanley Drunkenmiller and Kenneth Langone, the two billionaires on Geoffrey Canada's board of trustees. They realized, when Canada failed early on to get the test results his Robber Baron board members expected and Drunkenmiller told Tough (and undoubtedly Canada) that "the donors have every right to...divert their funds elsewhere," that the corporate quid pro quo was, after decades in the making, the universally accepted paradigm for nonprofits and schools and other social institutions. Every single Cornell Crew member, with the exception of Patrick McSweeney, accepted this corporate control of our destiny even though they were not at all sanguine about it but rather resigned to a fate over which they believed they had no control. It is a view that has been expressed by urban affairs experts like Dennis Judd who has observed that "life within some sort of corporation is what the future will increasingly be about." And if that is so, then nations and institutions alike will witness the continued decline and fall of civil society and democratic governance (Berman). We have certainly seen it in the little realm of our own institution, where democratic norms were not just degraded but disappeared entirely. One has to wonder, Patrick, if the public school in America, now beleaguered by both the federal government in the form of No Child Left Behind and by the corporate world's preference for privatization, will suffer the same fate.

The Nonprofit Executive as Corporate Philistine

We lack the intellectual resources to protect our institution from its slavish imitation of business.

Patrick, it was great to get together with you and Mary Margaret at our last Cornell Crew meeting in New York. I think our colleagues on the Crew were moved by your little dinner speech about the importance of keeping continuity with our traditions as a guidance and youth development institution. I, unfortunately, am a populist without a party, a rabble-rouser without a following—even among our closest friends and associates on the Cornell Crew—other than you of course. It was obvious I could not persuade them to reject the idea of being defined by donors, especially by a corporate class of billionaire businessmen. Our Crew colleagues lack, perhaps we all lack—as I indicated to you in an earlier letter—the broader and deeper curiosity that comes out of the humanities, out of the life of the mind that would enable us not only to protect and nurture the mission of our institution but also to reflect on its nature as a nonprofit. We lack, as busybody businessmen and women, the capacity for curiosity and reflection. We lack the intellectual resources to protect our institution from its slavish and coarse imitation of business. We are, sadly, too limited in our scope, too resigned in our spirit, and too enthralled in a larger culture that is vastly more corporate than civic in nature.

When I consider the rising generation of executives (I cannot bring myself to call them leaders) in our field and in other nonprofit fields, I fear that far too many of them are the equivalent of corporate philistines: they are incurious, unread, and unreflective. There are almost no true generalists, no liberally educated souls among them, which, in the nonprofit world I envision, ought to be the first, though not the only, requirement of leadership. We in the Youth Association International need a new generation of nonprofit leaders broadly educated in the humanities so that our vision of lifting generations of young people to a level of citizenship not seen since the founding of our nation can actually be something more than a marketing slogan. We need a generation of leaders that relates to the donor world and the public at large the way that independent artists of real integrity have historically related to the patron world, by first expressing their own vision, however unpopular or idiosyncratic that vision may be, in the quality of their work, then showing it to the potential patron for support rather than, as we and others have done, allowing the donor world to define us in bleak, pseudo-scientific terms. We simply lack the courage, the imagination, the broad background in the humanities and the depth of knowledge in human development (setting aside for a moment how daunting a fight it would inevitably be) to even make a compelling case for maintaining nonprofits such as ours as something other than base businesses, as, instead, social institutions deeply rooted in the best that has been thought and written about human and, in our case, child, development.

Higher education, having undergone a

similar corporatization of its purpose and culture, has been and will probably continue to be of little or no help in reimagining America's nonprofits as genuine social and educational institutions, as something more than corporate clichés. Even though the corporatization of colleges and universities may have taken longer than other centers of American life, perhaps due in part to the tenured intellectuals who resisted it, they are now dominated too by a business ethos that sees the traditional college president, one who had previously risen from the intellectual ranks of the humanities, as President and CEO.

In the last two centuries higher education has gone from cultivating a life of the mind to imparting skills and preparing people for careers; it has gone from asking profound questions about the meaning of life to prosaic ones like what is my major going to be, and its goal has gone from producing citizens who have an enlightened conception of the good life to producing workers who define the good life largely in material terms. Education has become a preparation for work rather than life, its end the economic life rather than the good life. If this is what "higher" education has become, Paddy, then it may not matter what happens to public education. The path from preschool to graduate school is likely to remain an increasingly narrow one, ending not in a highway wide and spacious but in a philistine footpath the width and breadth of a high-wire, from which we will all inevitably fall.

By way of postscript, Patrick, I should tell you that I finagled my way onto a panel of purported education experts (of which I obviously am not one) charged with the dubious task of offering analysis on the big buzz documentary called *Waiting For Superman*, a title drawn from a comment Geoffrey Canada made about growing up in Harlem. The finagle consisted of persuading the United Way, the agency sponsoring, though (wisely) not endorsing, the screening of the film, that they ought to include, in addition to the panel of experts—a charter school CEO, a public school district superintendent, a public school union president—a nonprofit executive, since, after all, charter schools like Canada's operate as nonprofits. I've already previewed the film, made by the academy award-winning filmmaker, Davis Guggenheim, the guy who did Al Gore's film, . This documentary has the off-kiltered tone and one-sided feel of a propagandistic defense of charter schools. I'll let you know how it goes.

Michael

I have read and reread your latest letter, Michael, and I am in agreement with your overall view that we need humanists leading our social and educational institutions. But don't you think that our Cornell Crew colleagues in a limited way represent the old university model that you like, at least in the sense that they came up through the ranks after being recreation workers and program directors before becoming executives? They may not have the grounding in the humanities that you're calling for, with degrees in recreation and phys ed and business and so on, but they first made their bones, like you and I did, as program workers. Kind of like the faculty members who rise to the presidency of a college or university. But, as you say, the younger execs in our field are not coming up in the same way. Their whole background is business, educationally, experientially, and absent some sea change in American culture in general and in our field in particular, these young turks are the dour face of the future.

The Privatizers of Public Education

Geoffrey Canada and Michelle Rhee, lionized as innovators of public education, never challenge the core assumptions of public education, nor do they offer anything new or innovative in its place.

Well, Patrick, the wait is over for *Waiting For Superman.* The morning after the screening of the film and the genius panel discussion that followed, a photograph of the panelists and an accompanying article appeared in our local *Times-News.* It was a rather large photograph on the front page of a section of the paper titled Learning, and in it was a gray-suited superintendent talking into a hand-held microphone, another gray-suited public school official (of the union variety) looking out at the assembled throng (mostly public school teachers, I was told), a golden-haired charter school CEO looking in at either the talking superintendent or me sandwiched between the two suits. Although I got no mention in the article itself (the school officials were all quoted), I was the white-on-white center of the photo—white shirt, white mustache, long wavy white hair—looking down professorially at the legal pad resting on my knee and jotting down some brilliant bit (only to me apparently) of polemical analysis.

The article was notable for its lack of any context at all for the film. I wonder if the reporter even saw the film but instead showed up for the panel discussion and developed his piece around the rather limited comments of the other three panelists on stage. The only thing he reported about the film itself, which he probably got from preview material, was that it had spurred a national debate among educators after first being screened at the 2010 Sundance Film Festival. His headline simply read, "Film Screening Sparks Discussion about Teachers, Parents."

What he could have and should have written by way of background is that those in the vanguard of the charter school movement—Geoffrey Canada, DC schools superintendent Michelle Rhee, and billionaire do-gooder and self-appointed education czar-in-chief Bill Gates—fervently believe that the public school system is broken and that the last best hope for reform rests with the privatization efforts of the charter school crowd. Thus the insight of my charter school colleague on the panel: "The major thing is it's all about choice." The union guy countered this by saying, "It's bigger than just choice; we have a generation that is not used to working as hard as they have to." I think he was talking about the kids, a la the Calvinist Canada. As a teacher's union official, I doubt that he'd make public statements about any dilatory behavior on the part of public school teachers.

As for the superintendent seated next to me, he pointed out, rightly I think, that any teacher would like to teach the five kids featured in the film, because in each case the parents of those kids were committed and involved in their children's education. The implied point of course is that many public school teachers, perhaps most, maybe all, have to deal with kids who are unwilling, unable, or both, and who have parents who are equally indifferent to and estranged from their children's education.

The only other point made in the article was the superintendent's defense of teacher tenure. Whereas the film argued that public schools don't succeed in part because union-protected teachers who are poor at their profession cannot be fired, the superintendent called this an unfair characterization of how tenure actually works in public schools. He said that the teachers in his district are continually judged on their classroom performance and are sometimes dismissed for underperforming. He also said that it shouldn't surprise anyone that some teachers are better than others. "Any profession," he said, "has a range of performance."

Nothing I apparently said that night—and I was given, as were the other panelists, an opportunity to make an opening and closing statement—was worth noting in the reporter's article. So let me burden you, an audience of one, with my polemics, Patrick. You're not a big audience obviously, but quite big in thought, in graciousness, in esteem. So here are my opening remarks, embellished just a bit for your edification.

Businesses are important institutions in American life. They create wealth. They create jobs. They engage in philanthropy. But when you apply business models to educational institutions, you inevitably get unintended consequences that are negative, even injurious.

Consider these examples:

Instead of broadening the purpose of public education from its preoccupation with career preparation to one which attends to the civic identities of children, the business reformers want public education to serve economic interests related to material prosperity. But using a business model to reform public education defines its purpose down to economic materialism. Who and what should define our philosophy of education and, by extension, define who and what we are as a culture and a nation are not business leaders and business culture, not donors and marketers and branders of products and services. What should define us educationally and philosophically is knowledge sufficient in its breadth and depth to conduce to a conception of the good life.

In the movie, Bill Gates defines citizenship in technocratic terms: the citizen as knowledgeable about science instead of the citizen as knowledgeable about democratic principles and civic life. In doing so, Gates and others not only accord social science an authority that even pure science doesn't have—asserting that standardized test scores are predictive of macroeconomic outcomes related to material prosperity—but also diminish the democratic principles necessary for civic culture to thrive. The first priority of the public school should be to attend to the civic identity of our children, secondarily to the economic interests of the nation, and lastly, if at all, to the interests of corporations, which in the 21st century have become nations unto themselves.

And then the corporatists that Gates represents want to hold teachers accountable for these pseudo-scientific outcomes. They believe that teachers are or should be the equivalent of business managers who actually get to pick the people who determine their success. But teachers, as we all know, have to take who comes through the classroom door, from the willing and able to the unwilling and unable. Unlike the business manager, teachers can neither hire nor fire the students they teach.

But what is really stunning about this movie is that there is virtually nothing in it about education. It's all about the economic and political arrangements surrounding public education: things like teacher tenure, merit pay, and metrics.

Geoffrey Canada and Michelle Rhee, lionized as innovators in education, have nothing new to say about education. They simply represent the idea that a business ethos rather than a civic ethos ought to drive public education. They never challenge the core assumptions of public education, nor do they offer anything new and innovative in its place. Their recurrent theme is that the system is broken.

Rather than "the system," I prefer the term "paradigm." A paradigm is a kind of worldview in which your core assumptions are implicit in the paradigm and invariably go unquestioned even as the paradigm starts to break down. Instead of seeing the paradigm as the problem, the tendency (in the case of public education at least) is to blame the players—the teachers first and foremost, but also the parents and the kids themselves. We should look instead at the core assumptions of the current paradigm.

Public education privileges teaching as a profession rather than an extension of the life of the mind, as an exercise in professional competence rather than a life-long expression of intellectual curiosity, as a job to be performed rather than a calling to be fulfilled.

It privileges teachers as specialists over teachers as generalists, analytical thinking over imaginative thinking, the critical over the synthetic, the cognitive over the psychological, the quantitative over the qualitative, the systematic over the idiosyncratic, conformity over curiosity, textbooks over great books, common space over individual space, and the student as worker (or technocrat) over the student as citizen.

Public education, with its fragmentation

into distinct academic areas lacking any interdisciplinary integration, privileges the narrowing rather than the broadening of a student's understanding. It privileges analyzing ideas over generating ideas, skills over knowledge, the dissemination of knowledge over the cultivation of individual talents or attributes, and knowledge over wisdom.

I concluded my introductory remarks by noting that the so-called reformers featured in this film don't disagree with any of the core assumptions of public education because they're not in any real sense reformers. They're privatizers pitching business bromides, and by privileging the material life over the civic life and pushing market ideas as the template of our social and educational institutions, they're driving out any common conception of the good life and diminishing the idea of civic life to a point where it will be impossible to sustain democratic institutions and democratic government.

Your profundity, Palermo, probably befuddled everybody in the hall, from the reporter to the teachers in the audience, as it initially befuddled me, who had the advantage of reading and rereading your remarks. But after a few readings and a few reflections, I can only say that the public education system is too moribund to challenge its own assumptions, of which, as you amply point out, there are many. It's too legally encumbered a system. The current charter crowd, as you like to call them, may not have an innovative answer but at least they're calling the question. As for democracy, hells bells, what are we talking about here? As you yourself said, we're like the Romans who traded republic for imperium, democracy for empire. But don't worry, Michael, we're gonna win anyway. We're gonna win.

The Privatization Paradigm

...will in the end obstruct a deeper and more fundamental reform of public education, one that could imaginatively issue in a new education paradigm.

Although I couldn't quite permit myself to say it publicly, Patrick, the documentary *Waiting for Superman* was really a work of propaganda in that it ignored the innumerable negative implications of charter school education. The charter crowd might, as you say, call the question, and in some later iteration might innovate what they like to call "the system" in a way that they're not now capable of, but thus far the negatives are piling up en mass. They're making a narrow educational purpose (careerism) even narrower (test-taking), legitimizing the deficiencies of social science, breaking down the universal common purpose of public education to educate all by segmenting kids who are motivated (into places like KIPP Schools) from kids who are not, demonizing teachers unfairly by falsely equating teaching with running a business, and tinkering at the margins of reform rather than challenging the core assumptions of the public school paradigm.

Overall, this privatization paradigm will in the end obstruct a deeper and more fundamental reform of public education, one that could imaginatively and innovatively issue in a new education paradigm. But this will require making explicit the core assumptions that are now implicit in public education and debating those assumptions democratically in open public forums and then having the courage to create a new paradigm, one that truly engages teachers and students in the life of the mind and philosophically follows Thomas Huxley's humanistic definition (from a scientist, no less) of an educated person: someone who knows something about everything and everything about something.

Contrast that with the technocrat Bill Gates who said, "People get panicked about the economic success of this country. One thing will determine that. We cannot sustain an economy based on innovation unless we have citizens well-educated in math, science and engineering. If we fail at this, we won't be able to compete in the global economy." This is Billionaire Bill at his boogeyman best, forewarning all of us globalized workers about the impending economic apocalypse, which, his obliviousness aside, has, in the name of globalization, already arrived. He seems to have missed the fact that globalization, which has ruthlessly and inequitably favored capital over labor (at least labor here in America), has contributed to his becoming enormously wealthy while the rest of us citizen humanists have either plunged into poverty or seen our middle class standing decidedly diminished.

Your humanist comrade-in-arms,
Michael

Scientific Consciousness

Quantifiability, and the deliberate act of viewing nature as an abstraction from which one can distance oneself, all open the possibility that Bacon proclaimed as the true goal of science: control.
~Morris Berman

Well, Patrick, let me tell you about a speech I gave to a group of insurance executives, in which I talked about, of all things, the scientific consciousness that you see not just in technocrats like Bill Gates but just about everywhere one looks. I traced its origins back to the Enlightenment and the Scientific Revolution, to thinkers like Descartes, Bacon,

Galileo, and Newton, all of whom (and consequently all of us) subscribed to a theory of knowledge in which truth could only be arrived at analytically and mathematically.

I'm embellishing things a bit for you, Patrick, because there were some things I could not very well say to these sticky-fingered insurance operators whose pockets I was there to pick. What I did not say is that the merchant-entrepreneurial class that came to power during the Renaissance "had an obvious affinity with the new arithmetical Weltanschauung" and, as a class, "glorified the effort of the individual" and "came to see in financial calculation a way of comprehending the entire cosmos, came to regard quantification as the key to personal success because quantification alone was thought to enable mastery over nature by a rational understanding of its laws" (Berman). So, by the 17th century, the Scientific Revolution "hammered out a new way of perceiving reality. The most important change was the shift from quality to quantity, from why to how," a distinction between fact and value that meant that science could "only tell us how to do something, not what to do or whether we should do it" (Berman). Morris Berman explained the shift this way:

> The universe, once seen as alive, possessing its own goals and purposes, is now a collection of inert matter, hurrying around

endlessly and meaninglessly, as Alfred North Whitehead put it. What constitutes an acceptable explanation has thus been radically altered. The acid test of existence is quantifiability, and there are no more basic realities in any object other than the parts into which it can be broken down. Finally, atomism, quantifiability, and the deliberate act of viewing nature as an abstraction from which one can distance oneself—all open the possibility that Bacon proclaimed as the true goal of science: control.

This scientific consciousness, this theory of knowledge, which unqualifiedly posits that "to know something is to subdivide it, quantify it, and recombine it; it is to ask how, and never get entangled in the complicated underbrush of why," remains our worldview to this day, leaving us to look at the world and any material thing in it as only "consisting of the sum of its parts, no more and no less" (Berman).

I realize I'm only scratching the epistemological surface of what Western philosophy (let alone Eastern philosophy) has to say about theories of knowledge, but I've digressed a bit to illustrate why it is important for the executives and the program people alike who run our Associations to know something about everything and everything about something so that when all this metric-minded nonsense is foisted on them by the crude scientism coming out of Whitehall, they have some intellectual resources and some historical context with which to judge it knowledgably and creatively. Otherwise they're lost; they have no ideas; they have no language with which to dissent.

As ever, dissenting,
Michael

The New Cosmology

That we must now constantly calculate things in a material world completely detached from our consciousness means that we can only conceive of things, even, in our case, children, in instrumental terms.

Patrick, picking up where I left off last time, let me just say there are deeper philosophical implications to this scientific shift in our thinking other than the epistemological ones that I previously mentioned, which of course I did not bother sharing with my insurance executive audience who probably thought that what I did have to say was rather odd to begin with but who were kind enough to give me thousands of dollars for our Youth Association anyway. But these deeper implications are on full display in Richard Tarnas's *The Passion of the Western Mind*, a beautifully rendered and lucidly argued one-volume intellectual history of the West.

In his book Tarnas argues that Copernicus was a pivotal figure in this shift in our consciousness that led to the preeminence of science over more spiritual and intuitive conceptions of reality. What Copernicus did in 1543 is supplant the earth as the center of the universe. This liberated humanity from its "geocentric illusion" but also "effected a cosmic displacement." The "Copernican effect," as Tarnas called it, set in motion a sense of "liberation while intensifying that displacement." The scientific liberation from religious dogma and spiritual superstition eventually led to a sense of alienation because now Western society had lost the traditional cultural context for "understanding the larger issues of human existence." And with "each succeeding step in the Scientific Revolution," new dimensions were added to the Copernican effect, bringing with them both an elevating sense of liberation and a diminishing sense of displacement. "The new universe was a machine…devoid of purpose," one in which "mind and matter, psyche and world, were separate realities." With figures like Galileo and Descartes and Newton, a new cosmology was forged that allowed the human intellect to act with greater freedom and effectiveness, but also meant that this new worldview would be characterized by a "disenchantment of all the spiritual qualities that for millennia had given human beings their sense of cosmic meaning." With "science's quantitative analysis of the world," humanity was "liberated from subjective distortions" but saw a diminishment of the very qualities that once constituted the human experience—"emotional, aesthetic, ethical, sensory, imaginative, intentional."

Finally, given that the rise of science occurred in conjunction with the rise of capitalism, it is not coincidental that the corporation is the template for modernity and for virtually all of our institutions, nor is it coincidental that "exact numerical calculation is the theoretical counterpart of a capitalist economy"(Berman). That we must now constantly calculate things in a material world completely detached from our consciousness means that we can only conceive of things, including people, even, in our case, children, in instrumental terms.

> Nature (including human beings) is seen as so much stuff to be grasped and shaped. Nothing can have purpose in itself...Reason is now completely (at least in theory) instrumental...One can no longer ask, 'Is this good,' but only 'Does this work?,' a question that reflects the mentality of the Commercial Revolution and the growing emphasis on production, prediction, and control (Berman).

However intellectually pretentious the above philosophizing may seem, Patrick, to the uninitiated business bros running our Associations and however remote ideas of displacement and alienation may seem to the "I feel happy, I feel terrific" slogans to which this can-do how-to crowd must inevitably subscribe, I think it is important for them to understand the rather deep and complex antecedents of our attachment to metrics, numbers, and data points and the other more concrete displacement it has brought to our doorstep, the one that means we cease being a youth development institution constituted to discover and nurture the many and varied talents of individual children and to forge secure attachments for them to caring adults. Our good friend Eileen Boyer's answer to this slippery slide into becoming a numbers-driven educational institution capable of collecting (I would not dignify it as measuring) data for the corporati is that we do all of it, which for practical purposes means, as Berman pointed out, the why will give way to the how, quality will give way to quantity, the idiosyncratic to the standardized, autonomy to control, and democratic process to corporate fiat. I say fuck the fiats, fuck the standards, and fuck the metrics, my good man.

Michael

The Numbers-Driven Nonprofit

Science must become a universal mathematics;
numbers are the only test of certainty.
~Descartes

Now where was I, Patrick? Ah, yes, my speech to a room full of insurance executives. I was saying to them that the Enlightenment and the Scientific Revolution left us with the idea that we can only explain something by breaking it down into its component parts, that there is no meaning beyond the parts. We can see evidence of this, I told them, in the donor world's preference for funding component parts of nonprofit agencies, what we familiarly call programs, instead of the whole entity or agency. We can see it in the way we approach education. Reading, which is essential to learning, is almost always taught and evaluated in analytical terms. Kids are rarely if ever taught or encouraged to read for ideas, which would put the value on idea generation, on synthesis instead of analysis, and might just have the effect of producing more innovators like Steve Jobs, whose genius, at least from the point of view of his biographer, Walter Isaacson, lay at the intersection of science and the liberal arts.

This supposed enlightened and scientific worldview begins with a belief with which we are now utterly enthralled, that numbers are the only test of certainty. It is an old idea. Inscribed above the entrance to Plato's Academy was the line: Let none ignorant of geometry enter here. From the Enlightenment you get figures like Rene Descartes saying that science must become a universal mathematics; that numbers are the only test of certainty. I mentioned the contemporary version of this, the Gatesian citizen as engineer, but it was my counterpoint to Gates from his billionaire buddy Warren Buffett that elicited loud laughter. It was the Oracle of Omaha who once wisely and wryly said, "If I needed calculus to make investments, I'd still be delivering newspapers in Omaha."

Since my elevated oratory that day was delivered with all the good-spirited acquisitiveness I could summon—as one must, as the agency's fundraiser-in-chief—I magnanimously conceded that the metric-mindedness that had so captured our imaginations and so definitively defined our worldview here in modernity had certainly served the corporate world well, providing companies like theirs with accountants and actuaries and assorted other numbers men and women who can count and recount the beans. The preoccupation with metrics applied to their business then, is, in its limited sense, understandable, but applied to our world, to child development, to the complexities of the human personality, is narrow to the point of irrelevance, and therefore has not served the nonprofit world well. It has put nonprofit agencies in a position of making claims in numerical terms that we can't legitimately make from a scientific standpoint, claims like having higher graduation rates or lower truancy rates or higher grade-point averages than public school students in general, claims that have the "certainty," to use Descartes term, of something equivalent to astrology. It forces people in our realm to give a certitude to social science that even pure science doesn't have.

If you look at the history of physics, for example, you see that every time science thought it understood the nature of reality, our understanding changed, whether it was Copernicus trumping Aristotle; Newton, Copernicus; Einstein, Newton; or Bohrs, Einstein. So whereas physics, which is ultimately based upon mathematical formalism and experimentation, has changed its view of reality many times over, with quantum mechanics and its probabilistic universe now the accepted view, social science simply "cannot expect the methods of science to work with equal precision or to command comparably broad assent when it comes to the study of human affairs" (Gaddis). The problem with social science commenting on the complexity of human affairs is that it "seeks to build universally applicable generalizations about simple matters; but if these matters are any more complicated" (like, say, the development of a child physically, psychologically, intellectually),"their theories wouldn't be universally applicable. Hence, "when social scientists are right, they too often confirm the obvious. When they don't confirm the obvious, they're too often wrong" (Gaddis).

So, I said to them, an agency like mine, if we want to be funded by an agency like the United Way, has to reinvent itself into one capable of making claims such as this: the kids who come to the Youth Association have higher grade-point averages than their peers at school, which, in John Lewis Gaddis's world does nothing more than confirm the obvious; that is to say, to attribute educational success of this kind to the efficacy of the Association's tutoring (as if one could really isolate that one variable) could just as easily be attributed to the likelihood that children motivated enough to attend an after-school youth development agency were also motivated to apply themselves to their schoolwork long before they ever walked into an Association facility. What this kind of argument really represents is the nonprofit world's imitation of another banality of the business world, public relations: the saying of simple slogans, in person, in print, in electronic media, that may or may not be true but are promulgated with enough business brio to convince its constituencies that they are, indeed, true.

Michael

For the Best Ideas to Prevail

If you want the best ideas to prevail, you have to read and reflect on the best that has been thought and written.
~Matthew Arnold

Allow me to add this, my good man, to my last letter: the educator Robert Birnbaum was wise when he noted that "those things of greatest value are precisely those things that cannot be measured; and if we cannot measure what is valuable, we will come to value what is measureable." Precisely what we've done, Paddy. Which is why we'll never find the answers to what is of greatest value to children just looking at science and math. The late Steve Jobs obviously understood this with his inclusion of the humanities in his own creative aesthetic. But the humanities unfortunately have been undergoing a steady devaluation since the scientific revolution began. A student entering Harvard two hundred years ago would have spent four years intellectually engaged with the question of what is the meaning of life. He would have understood what Kant meant when he wrote that "science is organized knowledge; wisdom is organized life." Students entering Harvard today are asking themselves more mundane questions, like what should my major be and what kind of career will it get me.

Matthew Arnold, the British poet and

literary critic who by profession was a school inspector, was once famous for having written that if you wanted the best ideas to prevail, then you must read and reflect on the best that has been thought and written. To consider the best that has been thought and written about human development, including, of course, child development, you'd want to start with the contrasting philosophies of Rousseau and Locke, then on to the psychoanalytic literature of Freud and Jung and Erickson, from there Bolby, Ainsworth, Bandura, Piaget, up to the current day with perhaps a David Hamburg or a Martin Seligman. And what would you find there? You would find, among other things, that what is preeminently important to the life chances of a child are secure attachments to caring adults and opportunities for mastery, neither of which lend themselves to measurement—perhaps identification, but not measurement. So we, the decision-makers, the staff and board, of the Youth Association (an institution historically dedicated to the things of fundamental value to a child) now find ourselves in the awkward and unenviable position of having to reinvent ourselves as an educational institution dedicated to a narrower, more limited set of values, which will ultimately attenuate our ability (with limited resources) to find every child's interest or talent and nurture it and inevitably diminish our ability to concentrate on those all-important connections between adult and child.

This is not to devalue education. No one values education more than I. Anyone who knows me well, Patrick, knows that I value the life of the mind. But academic ability is only one of many talents that can be nurtured in an Association program and facility, and if and when it becomes the only talent, a circumstance, given today's narrower preoccupations, that could come to pass, then we will have lost our way, we will have lost our ability to achieve the noble aspiration of improving the life chances of every single child who passes through public education's doors. So let's prevail, Patrick.

An Enlightened Philosophy of the Child

Looking at children through the prism of metrics reduces their humanity down to dull data points.

But how does one prevail, Patrick, in the standardized, stone-lined field of public education with its billionaire businessmen like Bill Gates, accountable to no one (certainly no citizens), who recently remarked that he has been "struck again and again by how important measurement is to improving the human condition," with successive federal regimes of No Child Left Behind that have led to a lockdown day prison system for children steeped in standards and measurements and fragmented specializations, teaching skills at the expense of teaching children to think, and becoming, as John Ralston Saul has observed, "handmaidens of the corporate system," with countless charter school opportunists looking to grab a piece of the five hundred and fifty billion dollar public school pie? How does one see this as other than the decline and fall of public education?

Charter schools, as currently constituted, are not the answer. The reformers behind the charter movement are not really reformers but radicals who simply want to bring a broken system down. In the end that may turn out to be their only significant accomplishment. The real challenge will be to replace the broken paradigm, the utterly moribund system, with something more than privatized prescriptions and Calvinist calls to long hours and hard work. The real challenge will be to come up with a new paradigm that posits a set of assumptions that are actually educational in nature but for now impossible to implement given current custom, byzantine legal parameters, special interest academic disciplines fighting furiously to maintain their place in the public education pantheon, and an overall bureaucratized corporate model resistant to anything other than paint-by-the-numbers, cookie-cutter core standards. Otherwise, one might ask why not public school teachers who are broadly educated rather than narrow content specialists and who regard teaching as an extension of the life of the mind rather than a credentialed career path? Why not teachers who teach twenty students from the students' first day of school until their last, instead of teaching one hundred and twenty different kids every day, year after year? Why not encourage kids to read for ideas rather than be bound by the narrow analytical approach inherited from the Enlightenment, respecting, as the poet Shelley advised, the similitudes of things? Why not encourage kids to discover an area of academic interest at the start of middle school, then broaden that interest over time by making connections to other disciplines as they go? This would of course require having teachers with the intellectual breadth and the wide-ranging curiosity to facilitate such a path. Why not change the spatial configuration of schools so that the kinds of spaces kids are educated in will mirror the spaces in which they will actually live and work in the future? And finally, why not a more enlightened philosophy of the child? Looking at children through the prism of metrics reduces their humanity down to dull data points and otherwise misuses them as means to organizational ends instead of dignifying them as artistic and humane ends in themselves. To witness what I mean by this, all the privatizers of public education would have to do is watch what happens to children at play through a more transparently humanistic prism, one clear of all the cant, and they would see children whose value and worth are independent of the results they produce, and who, in the pleasure of play, find pure joy and a glimpse of the divine.

Michael

You've given me a lot to ponder, Palermo. Too much, I'm afraid. Entering, like Lear, the winter of my years, I'm perhaps more confused than amused by life. I don't know where to begin to talk about your last letters and their big bag of ideas. It seems to be more disillusionment than liberation, fragmentation than amalgamation, parts than wholes. I was never much of an amalgamator, Michael. More of an analyzer, I'm afraid. I think your boys Berman and Tarnas are right, however, about this idea that just about everything we encounter, every thought that captures our consciousness, is a fragment of some whole that eludes us. Maybe you can pull the pieces of public education together, though, with your generalist-driven, interdisciplinary approach. I think you can win with that as your paradigm. I think you can, and I think you should.

Teachers: A Class of Specialized Bureaucrats

The more knowledge is limited to a single corner, the more ignorant the expert.
~John Ralston Saul

Okay, Patrick, but was it not Lear who asked, "Is man no more than this?" You are and have always been much more than just an analyzer, my friend. Your many ideas over the years solidified (and synthesized) a cultural understanding of the Association as a distinctly social institution that was designed to discover individual talents—whether they were social, psychological, physical or intellectual—and to nurture lasting relationships. As corporatization brought with it fragmentation and quantification and an overzealous preoccupation with pieces of program that could be marketed and sold to donors and funders, you and your contrarian contemporaries stood steadfastly for engaging kids in forging friendships with adults and peers and in evoking their natural curiosity in activities that interested them. You kept alive the idea that there was something noble and important and true about remaining a guidance and youth development institution instead of a more narrowly constituted supplementary education entity, that, beyond the mastering of prescribed information from a school curriculum, nurturing a child's curiosity could more creatively change the trajectory of a child's life, and that establishing the intimate bonds of friendship and of love could, as the philosopher Robert Nozick noted, "change the boundaries of the self and alter its topology."

That may be as close as we can get in modernity to seeing children as something other than students or future workers or tools to economic prosperity, instead of seeing them in their full humanity as good and gracious human beings—a phrase, oddly enough, used quite frequently by our friend Eileen Boyer—capable of a broad curiosity that is as much psychological as it is cognitive or intellectual and of an affinity for friendship and love, for, as it were, a more noble conception of the good life.

I think Richard Tarnas is, as you say, right about the fragmented nature of modernity, about the postmodern epistemological obsession with fragments or fractures. His view is that we have come to believe that "totalization in any human endeavor is potentially totalitarian," that "to think well, to feel well, to act well, to read well… is to refuse the tyranny of wholes." There is, therefore, no chance in the postmodern world of having a grand theory of things, of having any "comprehensive, coherent outlook" (Tarnas). "The postmodern paradigm is by its nature fundamentally subversive of all paradigms, for at its core is the awareness of reality as being at once multiple, local and temporal, and without demonstrable foundation" (Tarnas). "There are," as Nietzche observed, "no facts, only interpretations."

And since there are no facts, here is my interpretation. I don't think Thomas Kuhn, who coined the term "paradigm," would agree with Richard Tarnas that the postmodern paradigm is subversive of all paradigms. Paradigms, in spite our fragmented view of reality, do indeed form, just as one has formed around the idea of public education, and once formed they are stubbornly resistant to change. The public school of the twenty-first century, despite being a standardized system, does not have what Tarnas called a "comprehensive, coherent outlook." It has no fundamental philosophy that I can discern. It is a patchwork of Tarnas's fractures and fragments. It is a system, yes, but more of an assemblage of Nietzche's interpreted facts.

Bill Gates, for example, in a speech to state legislators, used the term "data" sixteen times, the term "standards" fifteen times, and referred to "measuring performance" twenty-two times. Whereas Gates and other charter advocates have tried to pass themselves off as innovative pragmatists purportedly trying to test new ideas in what they like to think of as a public education marketplace, what they have consistently migrated to is standardization, what we now call common standards. Standardizing everything is hardly a pragmatic approach to discovering what works best. It is a dogmatic corporatized approach that imposes a systemization of public education through data systems and their corresponding emphasis on quantification. It is an approach that would lead, as Max Weber observed a century ago, to the rise of a class of specialized bureaucrats (in this case, education bureaucrats) that Weber regarded as "specialists without a heart," as "monsters of effectiveness and efficiency increasingly lacking in any human vision or concern."

If "monsters" is wickedly overstated, "specialists without a heart" is not. Any approach to education, public or private, that defines children down to data points and quantifiable outcomes, is, especially when it is invoked in the context of institutional effectiveness and efficiency, dehumanizing. It has the effect of reducing children, as Marcuse would characterize it, to commodities, to skill sets, mathematical or otherwise, acquired by the system of public education and ultimately offered for sale to the lowest business bidder.

But this dehumanization of children doesn't emanate only from conforming to the deadening and unimaginative standards of fragmented educational systems or to the lowest common denominator efficiencies of business bureaucrats; it also comes from the teachers, specialists themselves, who are largely detached disseminators of information with neither the inclination nor the opportunity nor the breadth of understanding of the humanities to establish deep and meaningful connections to children. Like our fractured scientific consciousness, one in which "subject and object are always in opposition to each other" (Berman), always separate, always detached, teaching, when viewed strictly as a professional, academic exercise, encumbered as it is by state and federal laws and innumerable union rules and the disinterested stance that understandably follows from fears of child abuse, has largely become an exercise in emotional as well as intellectual detachment. Some teachers, certainly not all, care about the kids, but the obstacles to connect with them in a meaningful way in the context of the current paradigm are too formidable to overcome.

Fragmentation, and the disconnect it engenders, abounds in elementary and high school education, public and private. It starts with teachers, mere content specialists, who cannot, by virtue of their specialized education and the specialized teaching assignments that the bureaucratized system insists upon, make connections to other disciplines that might meaningfully impart a breadth of learning to the children they teach. Teachers, however permanent their positions, however long their tenure in any one teaching position, are like anchors to which their students are temporarily tethered: each year brings a new vessel, a new crew of kids who sail off into the sunset, or into the impending storm, at the end of each school year. Been sailing ever since.

Michael

Towards an Evolving Canon of Content

The idea would be to proceed as Matthew Arnold thought we should proceed, with each generation seeking to discover the best that has been thought and written, then offering that living canon not as a prescription but as an ever evolving framework for every child's education.

Ah, yes, about the content of education, that field of battle full of foxholes and barbed wire, a few observations, Mr. McSweeney. With each discipline making a claim to a canon of content, the assembled knowledge from the various disciplines—math, science, history, literature, and so on—then becomes, presumably, the prescribed canon in toto. Writing in the 1980's, the educator E.D. Hirsch, Jr. argued in effect for a canon of content based on cultural literacy, on the anthropological idea that "all human communities are founded upon specific shared information." Contrasting the education philosophies of Plato and Rousseau,

Hirsch came down solidly on the side of Plato's concept of education, at least to the extent that "the specific contents transmitted to children are by far the most important elements of education" (Hirsch). Hirsch quoted, from Plato's *The Republic*, this comment from Socrates: "Shall we carelessly allow children to hear any casual tales which may be devised by casual persons, and to receive into their minds ideas for the most part the very opposite of which we shall wish them to have when they are grown up?" Hirsch then added that Plato had "good reasons for being concerned with the specific contents of schooling," one of them being ethical, and quoted the master, the foundational philosopher of the West, once more: "For great is the issue at stake, greater than appears—whether a person is to be good or bad."

I quite understand, Patrick, why Hirsch would side with the political and intellectual perfectionist (one might say absolutist) Plato rather than the more individualistic and relativistic Rousseau. If your position is, as Hirsch would have it, that a cultural canon exists and that it ought to be imparted to children as a part of their education, as part of their intellectual make-up as a citizen of a particular state, then a philosopher like Plato, who metaphysically believed that every idea existed in its essence in the more perfect world of Forms and therefore believed that Truth existed with a capital T, is, indeed, your man, mentor, muse.

The problem with Hirsch's position is that Plato the elitist left out of his utopian (or dystopian) educational vision the farmers and traders and artisans. The whole idea of a cultural canon is that it is to be universally disseminated as part of a public system. The contemporary equivalent of Plato's meritocratic approach can be found in the work of conservative public policy thinkers like Charles Murray who believe that the main premise of public education, that every single child can and ought to achieve at least a proficient level of educational success, is foolishly romantic. Some kids, many perhaps, cannot and will not succeed, in Murray's view. Murray the meritocrat, the elitist, would instead frame our educational future by concentrating our efforts on the best and brightest, on the kids who will one day lead the major institutions of our nation, insisting that they be broadly educated in the liberal arts so they would know and understand, among other things, among many other things, Plato's concept of the Good.

But there's something disingenuous in invoking Plato to defend the idea that the dissemination of information, of "specific content," in the interest of coalescing a community around the idea of a shared literacy, is the fundamental purpose of education. Even

Hirsch's own reference to ethics reveals Plato's real educational purpose, which is to give those guardians who have risen to the level of Ruler the authority to censure the stories, the poetry, the educational content that does not contribute to the truthful and proper molding of character. "It seems, then," Socrates said to Adeimantus, "our first business will be to supervise the making of fables and legends, rejecting all which are unsatisfactory; and we shall induce nurses and mothers to tell their children only those which we have approved, and to think more of molding their souls with these stories than they now do of rubbing their limbs to make them strong and shapely" (Plato).

Is there a substantive difference in the censorship practiced in Plato's *Republic* and that of modern-day educational policymakers like E.D. Hirsch, Jr.? Other than one having a moral intention and the other more of a communitarian intention, both visions are rooted in the idea that the wise, whether rulers of an ancient republic or policymakers in a twenty-first century empire, can and do know what's best for the education of its citizens. There is something noble, idealistic, even utopian, in the attempt to arrive at a complete and categorical understanding of what constitutes the substance of not just anyone's, but everyone's, education. Both the ancient philosopher Plato and the modern university professor Hirsch then want to prescribe a categorical understanding of what the substance of education actually is, but differ radically in substance and purpose. For Plato the overall purpose of education is a moral aspiration to a higher life based upon knowing the Good with a capital G (i.e., to know the Good is to do the Good), and his concept of the content of education, liberally and classically broad—reading, writing, poetry, arithmetic, geometry, music, art and philosophy—was only prescriptive from a moral perspective.

Hirsch, taking an anthropological view, "stresses the universal fact that a human group must have effective communications to function effectively," that effective communications require shared culture, and that shared culture requires transmission of specific information. The purpose of education then is to have a human group, a society, "function effectively" as a shared culture, and its substance, its "specific information," is to be definitively prescribed and universally promulgated; thus the subtitles of Hirsch's book are "what every American needs to know," and "includes 5,000 essential names, phrases, dates, and concepts." Hirsch tried to make the distinction, disingenuously I think, that his notion of cultural literacy did not mean a prescriptive canon of books "but rather a descriptive list of the information actually possessed by literate Americans," and his aim was simply to "make that information the possession of all Americans." Not only is having everyone possess the same information prescriptive, it is an outlook, given the globalized, hyper-informational world that emerged since the publication of Hirsch's book and its advancement of this anthropological thesis, that seems quite quaint now, perhaps superfluous, even bizarre, though in fairness he did qualify his overreaching assertion with this commonsense caveat: "But even the greatest thinkers, being human, see mainly in one direction at a time, and no thinkers, however profound, can foresee the future implications of their ideas when they are translated into social policy." The thinkers Hirsch was referring to in the context of this comment were Plato and Rousseau, but in retrospect he may well have been referring, rather presumptively, and perhaps even unconsciously, to himself.

The important point here, Paddy, is that, with the ubiquitous common culture that emerged here in America and around the world in the last few decades, a common culture driven by mass media and marketing and by the ever more rapid development and proliferation of information technology, there has never been in our history a more urgent need to fashion an education philosophy that is Rousseauian in its roots, from its content to its purpose. Hirsch, in arguing that education had been dominated by a content-neutral approach that sided with Rousseau's more individualistic emphasis on the natural development of children, created a straw man that ignored the fact that education in America has been dominated for decades by the prescriptions of curriculum developers and textbook writers and the metric standardization of education bureaucrats. Even if you mastered Hirsch's five thousand facts, and declared yourself literate, the real shared culture in America was long ago redefined by media images, advertising slogans and the minimalist data of emails and phone texts. Writing in the late eighties, around the same time that Houghton Mifflin published Hirsch's *Cultural Literacy*, the art critic Robert Hughes observed even then that the medium of television tended "to abort the imagination by leaving kids nothing *to* imagine," and with "a fine-arts culture given over to information and not experience," what we were now witnessing was "the reign of mere unassimilated data instead of events that gain meaning by being absorbed into the fabric of imaginative life." Hughes's sentiment, meaning grounded in experience rather than unassimilated data, is vintage Rousseau.

The antidote to the clichéd culture consigned by mass media lies somewhere between the moral and intellectual aspirations of classical antiquity and the more relativistic view of post-Enlightenment modernity. In that sense, Hirsch was right in asserting that "there is much truth in the durable educational theories of both Rousseau and Plato," thus suggesting that there might be a way of synthesizing the two polar philosophies of education: Plato's prescriptively moral, Rousseau's individualistically (i.e., the cultivation of one's natural tendencies) moral, Plato's (and Hirsch's) content- specific, Rousseau's content-neutral. Virtue then, not information, not culture, is the ultimate end of both classical theories, though the question of information, at least to the extent that we will inevitably be confronted with the ideas and information contained in the books and essays and articles and poems and stories from antiquity to the present, cannot in good conscience be ignored.

Information, mechanistically known today as data, will continue to flourish in our technological modernity, proliferating geometrically. We can count on the marketers and various mass media to parse it down for us to slogans and taglines, the impact of which, sadly, may very well be as great or even greater than that of a formal education. The problem with protecting children from it is that it is ubiquitous, and it puts one in the platonic position of censuring the informational world of a child. Still, some parents may opt to at least partially restrict television viewing, internet access and cellular phone use.

The question for educators is what to make of the information that finds its way into books and other forms, thus formulated as knowledge, as contenders for the canon or content of education. I have to say that in one respect I agree with Hirsch: we do need, if not a broad consensus, at least an on-going debate about the content of education, but one based on a canon of great books rather than Hirsch's five thousand facts. I would regard this canon, however, as a general framework around which every generation of educators and intellectuals could debate its merits. The idea would be to proceed as Matthew Arnold thought we should proceed, with each generation seeking to discover the best that has been thought and written, then offering that living canon not as a prescription but as an ever-evolving framework for every child's education, knowing that the perfect canon will probably elude every generation, though the pursuit if it is integral to living the life of the mind. And within that framework of an evolving canon of content, children could, indeed should, be encouraged to construct their own knowledge both deep in its penetration and broad in its reach. Classic Rousseau.

Michael

The Ultimate Purpose of Public Education

I didn't set out to have a career; I set out to have a life.
~Tilda Swinton

Patrick, the beauty of a living cannon of great books as the framework of a child's education is that it would be too broad and too textured to permit the full imposition of standardized curriculums by education bureaucrats, and it would be too protean and too idiosyncratic to permit the equally egregious imposition of dull textbooks by a corporate- controlled textbook franchise. A canon of this kind would move education away from the kind of universal prescription of content that Hirsch advocated toward a more flexible framework of the kind that Thomas Huxley articulated when he said that what we ought to know is something about everything and everything about something. Positing the importance of both breath and depth as general propositions, without prescribing either in definitive detail, would provide the urgent antidote and counterbalance to the corporate media that, in Robert Hughes' view, "drains the world of meaning." It would restrain attempts to narrow the purpose and content of education to measuring, through standardized tests, specialized knowledge in subjects like math and science, and therefore ignoring, as Diane

Ravitch warned, the moral and aesthetic goals of the humanities and the liberal arts. It is in the humanities and the liberal arts, Ravitch noted, that one can find the "personal qualities that we hold dear—resilience and courage in the face of stress, a sense of craft in our work, a commitment to justice and caring in our social relationships, and a dedication to advancing the public good in our communal life..."

All of the values that Ravitch mentioned, from resilience and courage, craft and commitment, justice and caring, to advancing the public good, are implicitly moral in their meaning. They are part of the moral make-up of the citizens of a society, in our case a democratic society, but one that has paradoxically wavered in its commitment to the Good, to the common good, or, simply, to the good life. Instead, throughout our history, we have remained neutral on the question of the good life (Sandel). We are more concerned with "toleration" and "fair procedures" and "individual rights" than we are with the "moral excellence of our citizens" (Sandel). And if our identities cannot be defined, at least in part, by participation in a common good, then there are no grounds on which to base the obligations of citizenship, and we are left with a procedural republic rather than a truly democratic one, a society that asserts the Right over the Good (Sandel).

But if one assumes that our public schools have been complicit in the failure to impart a conception of the good life to which a majority of Americans could subscribe, then it seems even less likely that the privatization efforts of charter schools will do any better and may indeed do much worse. Michael Sandel sees this as the "expansion of market-oriented reasoning into the spheres of life traditionally governed by non-market norms" to the point that we're "letting the market rewrite the norms that govern social institutions." Whereas Sandel is concerned with social institutions in general, Diane Ravitch directs her displeasure at the privatization of the public school. "Business leaders like the idea of turning the schools into a marketplace," she writes, "where the consumer is king. But the problem with the marketplace is that it dissolves communities and replaces them with consumers. Going to school is not the same as going shopping." Morris Berman is equally blunt about this: "Community life has been reduced to shopping malls."

The business leaders Ravitch is writing about include billionaire philanthropists who are having a huge impact on the privatization of public education, principally Bill Gates, Eli Broad and the Walton family, all of whom have foundations that are making "targeted investments" in elementary and secondary education. Unlike, say, the Annenberg

Foundation, which gave grants to organizations "to do as they thought best," the Gates, Broad and Walton foundations "treated their gifts as an investment that was expected to produce measureable results" (Ravitch). They supported "reform strategies that mirrored their own experience in acquiring huge fortunes, such as competition, choice, deregulation, incentives, and other market-based approaches" (Ravitch). The fundamental question this raises with Ravitch is whether it is wise to allow education policy to be "captured by private foundations" that are "run by society's wealthiest people" who "represent an unusually powerful force that is beyond the reach of democratic institutions." However noble their intentions, these foundations are not, Ravitch notes, institutions "subject to public oversight" or to the "scrutiny of voters" who could "vote them out of office" if they "didn't like the foundations' reform agenda." The irony is that while these "foundations demand that public schools and teachers be accountable for performance, they themselves are accountable to no one" (Ravitch), except perhaps a board of directors which they may or may not have hand-picked themselves. This is precisely what Sandel meant by democratic norms being degraded, even eliminated, when market norms come to dominate social institutions like the public school.

I'll close with this point, Patrick. The ultimate purpose of public education ought to be more than just knowing (even if it is done with both breadth and depth) as much as one can of the best that has been thought and written. Since the true measure of any society is what kind of people come to populate it, then our schools and our colleges and universities ought to know who and what their students should be when they pass through academe's door into the wider world. In a society defined more in market than moral terms, it might be sufficient to produce people prepared for careers and consumerism. In a society defined more by civic obligations than procedural rights, the purpose of education might be to produce citizens more interested in the pursuit of happiness than the pursuit of pleasure. In a society defined by a political and cultural consensus on the nature of the good life, education's end may be, to borrow Eileen Boyer's phrase, a society mostly of good and gracious human beings.

In the course of an interview, the actor Tilda Swinton was asked why she set out to have a career in acting. Her answer, which she gave without the slightest pause or reflection, as if it came not just from her mind but from her very being, was stunning, unforgettable: "I didn't set out to have a career," she said. "I set out to have a life."

And that, my friend, is what every kid in our

schools should be set on a path to do: have a life.

Give my best to Mary Margaret,
Michael

I do indeed like what you have to say about the larger purpose of public education, Palermo, but as time passes I keep wondering about what's going on at Whitehall with all the governance stuff. Is anything happening on that front?

The Good Things a Good Life Contains

Love and Friendship First

If anything is going on at Whitehall with, as you say, the governance stuff, it's going on quietly and, I'd like to think, uneventfully. They can't possibly be worried that our Pennsylvania Proposal, which they keep calling The Erie Proposal, will actually garner enough votes to be passed by the International Council. The only audience I've had, though it was a fairly significant one, about a thousand executives and board presidents, was at the last international conference, months ago. I have otherwise honored my understanding with Denny McAndrew and Eileen Boyer not to politic the proposal aggressively. They seemingly have held up their end of this uneasy suspension of hostilities.

But I have heard from them since I wrote you last. Denny called, for Eileen of course, who apparently wanted to know if I was mad at her, to which I told Denny, I'm not at all mad at her; I understand her and the corporate control imperative that defines her perfectly. Denny then told me Eileen wanted to hear from me. A date and time was arranged, I called her, and we talked, not about our antithetical political positions but about a friendship three decades deep. This is the human side to an otherwise stoic, businesslike persona that one rarely sees from our old friend Eileen, and it is a reminder to me that friendship, if it is true and good and genuine to the core, is unconditional and unassailable, no matter the depth of discord. And it is also a reminder of the good things a good life contains: love and friendship first, then the meaningful doing of one's work, whether that is changing the trajectory of a child's life or writing something that might be worth remembering and being reflected upon, then the books and ideas of a life of the mind, and finally the simple joys of food and drink in the company of loved ones and friends.

As for our friendship, let me leave you with this from the great Latin poet Titus Lucretius Carus, known to us of course as Lucretius, author of one of the greatest philosophical poems from classical antiquity, *On The Nature of Things*:

> But nothing is more blissful than to occupy the heights effectively fortified by the teaching of the wise, tranquil sanctuaries from which you can look down upon others and see them wandering everywhere in their random search for the way of life, competing for intellectual eminence, disputing about rank, and striving night and day with prodigious effort to scale the summit of wealth and to secure power.

So, thank you, Mr. McSweeney, for fortifying me with your own ways of wisdom for the life journey, still unfinished, now modeled in part after Lucretius' life of quiet tranquility.

Ciao,
Michael.

5

The Triumph of Corporate Culture

The form of government turns upon where legitimacy lies.
~John Ralston Saul

Vetting over Voting

The corruption of democratic norms has confirmed a form of governance in which vetting triumphs over voting.

Well, Paddy, you asked me not long ago what was happening at Whitehall with the governance stuff, and I wrote to you that it appeared nothing much at all was happening. Things were quiet and I hoped, or you might say speculated, that they were uneventful, too. I was, I realize now, to borrow a phrase from John Stuart Mill, a fool satisfied, when I should have remained like Socrates, decidedly dissatisfied. I had been speculating for months, as you know from our conversations, on how the international organization was going to handle having the Pennsylvania Proposal on the agenda of the International Council Meeting, not simply for a preliminary reading, but for a vote. Their problem is that nothing that has come before the Council in more than a decade has received anything but a blissfully ignorant and perfunctorily affirmative vote. If that happens again, we will have put in place a new governance structure, bicameral rather than unicameral, with a council controlled by Whitehall and a senate controlled by representatives from the field, thus reinstating what we once had and only relatively recently lost: democratic governance. We got our answer today, in the notice for the International Council Meeting, a thirty-page paean to political obfuscation and corporate cunning sent to the field from the secretary of the international board, Anne Hopkins. I've enclosed the whole dissembling document for you to look at, along with a few preliminary observations from one now abundantly dissatisfied:

This meeting notice is amateurish, intentionally misleading, and an exercise in dissembling rather than good governance.

All of the agenda items up for a vote (except one, The Erie Proposal) allow for a yes or no vote from the voting member (local) organizations.

The so-called Erie Proposal has instead been cunningly consolidated with another governance proposal that the international organization cooked up through its supposedly independent International Council Committee, all under the rubric of "changes to the International Council structure," with "only one yes vote allowed."

This International Council Committee, made up of, as you well know, about twenty board volunteers from local Youth Association organizations, is hand-picked by Whitehall and wined and dined and carefully facilitated by senior international staff, including Eileen. There is not an independent bone in that entire twenty-person body. In the roughly fifteen-year history of this committee (the creation of which no one seems to know anything about), it has never once taken a position at odds with Whitehall. Yet because it has local organization representation, it's passed off by Whitehall as a committee from the field, of which it patently is not.

The Committee's, or I should say Whitehall's, governance proposal, which voting delegates from the local organizations will be compelled to vote for or risk losing pass-through funding from Whitehall, is a veritable cornucopia of undemocratic ideas, from giving the International Council Committee (i.e., Whitehall) the exclusive responsibility of determining (they referred to it as vetting) what gets on the agenda for International Council

Meetings to allowing "electronic means of participation" (I guess you can't legitimately call it voting) that "reflects best practices of governance" (by whom?) and "additional means of proxy voting" (another supposed "best practice"), and which, taken together, really amount to a rather cynical exercise of civic disengagement.

Lastly, I would just say that consolidating the two governance proposals–one proposing changes to how the International Council operates and one adding an entirely new governance entity (the senate) to our constitutional structure–under the aegis of "changes to the International Council structure" was a deviously ingenious way to ensure that the senate idea could not possibly prevail. They, Whitehall, cavalierly decided that the two proposals were mutually exclusive, when one reasonably and legitimately could have voted for both.

So two months till the International Council Meeting officially convenes, and the cause—I suppose always a lost cause—already definitively decided. What power we once had, we ceded to Whitehall over the years in a long steady drift toward disengagement with governance. We contented ourselves with the idea that it was better to be a business than a social institution; better to be a standardized, corporatized brand than a youth-serving institution with a guiding philosophy and a few core principles; better to be a top-down corporation than a bottoms-up democratic institution. With the establishment of a senate, the power and legitimacy to govern, now so definitively concentrated at Whitehall, could once again have been shared. But that day has passed, Paddy. I am reminded of Lord Acton's fundamental insight: that power corrupts and absolute power corrupts absolutely. I would simply say that power without wisdom, without fairness, is sure to corrupt, and this corruption of democratic norms confirms a form of governance in which vetting triumphs over voting, customer relations over democratic participation, and corporate power over democratic legitimacy.

Michael

Dear Michael,

I'm afraid our Patrick is not well enough to write. I want you to know, however, that I read your last letter to him and he sends you, as always, his best. Ever the optimist, he says you're going to win, but I must say your challenge seems to be a formidable one. Good luck to you, Michael. And please keep writing us. It's good tonic for an old Irishman's soul.

Love,
Mary Margaret

The End of Engagement, the Beginning of Silence

The stark reality is that the kind of governance now offered to us does not privilege voice; it silences it. And it does not privilege real civic engagement; it effectively ends it.

Dear Mary Margaret,

I hope when you receive this letter Patrick is having one of his better days, in which case you could perhaps remind him of the many times he told me that to take an unpopular stand; even if there was not much prospect of persuading a single soul, it was still a noble thing to do. Conversely, you might also tell him that I'm no longer sure I'm fighting this fight for the right reasons, that maybe it's more to do with willfulness and a long-standing desire to defy authority. However uncertain my motivation may be, I've put too much thought and passion into this fight not to finish it. The only alternative now left to me is to publicly politic the issue in a way that I once promised Denny McAndrew and Eileen Boyer I would not do. The shameful way in which Whitehall jerry-rigged the upcoming vote on our governance proposal betrayed the trust on which that promise was based, and it has led me to draft the attached letter to send to every executive director of every local Youth Association organization. Tell Patrick I'll keep him posted with future letters from the front.

My Very Best,
Michael

Dear Colleagues:

I'm writing today to encourage you to vote for The Erie Proposal, one of two governance proposals on the agenda of this year's International Council Meeting. If approved, The Erie Proposal would establish—*in addition to* the International Council—an International Senate, thus creating a bicameral governance structure for the Youth Association International Movement. But before I comment on the proposal itself and the issues surrounding it, I'd like to tell you about my personal history with the Movement and my involvement with The Erie Proposal.

Background

I was a member of the Erie Youth Association in the 1960s, and I've been the executive director of the Erie organization since 1991. Prior to that date I was the executive director in Binghamton, New York, and before that I worked in the international headquarters of the Youth Association International in the Program Development Department.

In the last twenty years I've served on numerous national and international task forces, committees and commissions, most recently on the Centennial Commission and the International President's Advisory Council. In 2005 I was the recipient of the Harold K. Harte Character and Leadership Award from our international organization. For several years I served as a speechwriter for our International President, Eileen Boyer, my former boss at the international organization.

In my several decades of involvement in the Movement, I've had the privilege to experience the Association from many different vantage points: as a youth member and an alumnus, as a youth worker and an Association administrator, as a local executive and an international administrator, and as a supporter of our international organization to my current status as an outspoken critic of our national organization's approach to governing the Movement.

It has not been easy taking this critical stance with old friends and colleagues. I have sometimes felt as though I have been a loyal opposition of one, though I am heartened that others have begun to notice the steep decline in the civic quality and democratic nature of our governing entity, the International Council.

As the author of The Erie Proposal and a principal architect of it along with staff and board from my local organization, executives and board members from the Pennsylvania Area Council, and colleagues from my executive leadership group, the Cornell Crew, I'm committed to our proposal being fairly and accurately represented to the field. In the March notice announcing the International Council Meeting in New York there were substantive omissions and serious misrepresentations in the way that The Erie Proposal was described.

Omissions and Misrepresentations

On page eleven of the meeting notice, The Erie Proposal is described as proposing "the establishment of an International Senate as the governing entity for our Movement." What we actually proposed in the letter that appears on page twelve is the International Senate as *an additional governing structure as part of our constitutional structure,* not *the* governing structure of the Movement.

In several other instances our proposal is characterized as a change in the International Council structure. It actually does nothing of the kind. Instead it creates a second governing structure to go along with the International Council, but does not propose or even imply eliminating or changing the International Council itself. Our letter specifically states that "...we wish to make it clear that an International Senate is not being proposed as a replacement of the International Council, but rather an addition to it..." But by linking the two proposals under one agenda item as purported changes to the International Council, the false (dissembling would be more bluntly accurate) dichotomy is created that the two proposals are mutually exclusive; that a yes vote for one necessitates a no vote for the other. The Erie Proposal actually was very carefully crafted so you could in fact vote affirmatively for both governing proposals.

In addition to the fact that the two governance proposals are falsely and manipulatively linked under the rubric of changes to the International Council, they are formatted, quite unfairly, in radically different ways. The International Council Committee's proposal is formatted to look like constitutional changes to be added to the framework of our constitution, whereas as The Erie Proposal, which quite easily could have been put into constitutional language and formatted to look like constitutional changes, was left in the form of the letter that initiated it.

As for the reasons for supporting these governance proposals, the disparity of treatment was even more apparent. Whereas several reasons are given to support the international organization's governance proposal, not a single reason is offered in support of the only constitutional proposal to come from the field in almost three decades. So let me offer you just a few of the reasons why you ought to support it:

Governing power would be shared through a separation of powers, with the international organization controlling the International Council and the field controlling the International Senate.

A senate would for many reasons make our organization a democratic institution once again, not least because it would require actual majorities to change our constitution, not just majorities of quorums, potentially as little as thirteen percent of the field.

The senate would also give us, the field, a permanent national stage on which to exchange ideas, debate, and govern, whereas the alternative is to be governed by facilitated and scripted focus groups, hand-picked commissions, and electronic chat rooms.

A senate would at least partially reestablish our identity as community-driven social institutions with a fair measure of local autonomy, not just a "consistent system of local organizations" and a brand-driven corporation with command and control from the top.

And it is neither accurate nor fair to characterize the involvement of the field in the review process as open town hall meetings when they were actually facilitated focus groups, scripted and controlled by our international organization. It is certainly difficult, then, in view of the many omissions and outright misrepresentations, not to see the governance information contained in the meeting notice and the tightly controlled process that led to it as lacking a sense of proportion and fairness, and it raises the question of how this process might have been handled fairly, ethically, transparently.

What Could Have Been Done

The Erie organization or the Pennsylvania Area Council could have been asked to explain the reasons for establishing an International Senate, and this information could have been included in the notice announcing the International Council Meeting.

The Erie Proposal could have been fairly represented for what it actually is: a separate constitutional amendment that deserved to be listed as a separate item on the agenda of the International Council Meeting.

And strategies could have and should have been explored to reinvigorate a real civic engagement in the governance of the Movement, instead of diminishing it with "best practices" that actually disengage us rather than engage us.

Real Civic Engagement

The ultimate irony of our current approach to governance is that, while we tout civic engagement and citizenship development as a vision statement for the Movement, we have presided over the devaluation of the civic nature of our governance, essentially ending the open public square we once had in the

International Council, replacing it with a civic disengagement characterized by corporate practices like proxies, electronic voting and governance by chat room.

For those of you too young to remember what our International Council once was, I can only say that our meetings were never perfunctory two-minute exercises conducted at conference general sessions nor hastily adjourned meetings conducted later by electronic chat room. They were meetings that on occasion lasted at least a half day in which we met with each other in person as our founders intended and where we debated and discussed our governance issues face-to-face in a real public square.

We don't have to have our role in governance diminished to that of a shareholder in a big corporation. We can once again become stakeholders in a federation by voting for the International Senate and reestablishing a public square and a civic engagement commensurate to our vision as an institution. The stark reality is that the kind of governance now offered to us does not privilege voice; it silences it. And it does not privilege real civic engagement; it effectively ends it.

Dear Michael,

I read your last letter to Patrick, and though he was not well enough to write, he gave you the old

McSweeney thumbs up. We know that the International Council Meeting in New York is coming up very soon and we want you to know that we'll be thinking of you and hoping that your democratic proposal prevails. Know that we send our unwavering support and the very best we have to offer.

Love,
Mary Margaret

Stakeholders Not Shareholders; Citizens Not Customers

We, the local Association organizations, were once the equivalent of citizens in a democracy, and because of that the legitimacy of our governance rested with us.

Dear Patrick and Mary Margaret,

As I'm sure you've surmised, the attempt, I suppose quixotic at its core, to bring back democratic governance to an institution which we have long loved and to which we have devoted our lives did not, as I and the two of you had hoped it would, prevail. I don't know what the actual final tally was—since most of the votes were proxies or were cast electronically at unattended computer voting stations in and around conference meeting rooms before and after the International Council Meeting—but Denny McAndrew tells me that our proposal garnered about five percent of the roughly four hundred votes cast.

The meeting itself was conducted in a relatively large room with every seat taken and delegates standing two deep in the aisles on the perimeter. Also standing, but on a raised platform behind an imposing podium, was the even more imposing chairman of the international board, Edward Holbrook, lean, lambent, and preternaturally composed. After calling the assembled to order, he prefaced the business portion of the meeting with his own paean to democracy's due process, stressing that every attempt had been made to encourage all member organizations to exercise their right to vote whether in person or by proxy or at one of the electronic stations strategically located around the site of the conference. And as long as one stipulates the ethically uncomfortable fact that they fund the local Association organizations whose votes they are soliciting and if one further stipulates the fact that Whitehall only allots a half hour for the Council Meeting to ensure that we have no real stage on which to have an open dialogue, then this expansive approach to voting seems noble to the point of magnanimity.

The meeting, an exemplar of brevity and corporate expedience, was dominated by two presentations: one by a member of the International Council Committee explaining and touting Whitehall's governance proposal and one by me advancing the first proposal from the field of any kind in three decades. Since Cool Hand Holbrook did not introduce me as a formal part of the agenda but did introduce the Council Committee member for his report, I had to seize my opportunity near the end of the meeting (but before the so-called vote) when Holbrook opened the floor for comments or questions. After introducing myself as the author of the letter that recently went out to executive directors defending The Erie Proposal, I told my dutifully assembled colleagues from the field that I wanted to make a few general observations, reaffirm a few points made in my letter, and read a few passages from a book that I thought was relevant to our identity as a democratic nonprofit institution.

This is what I said:

My first general observation today is that our international organization cannot both fund local organizations while it controls every aspect of our governance—from convening, presiding, setting the agenda, and keeping the records—without acknowledging that its conflict of interest is a breach of ethics and of public trust, without seeking a remedy to this obvious ethical conundrum. If we had a senate, however, in which the power to govern was shared with the field, that conflict of interest would be decidedly diminished and, one could argue, largely remedied. Under our current structure of governance, that vitally important ethical issue will never come before us for our consideration. In fact, without a senate, this will undoubtedly be the last time you'll even hear it mentioned in any public forum of our international organization.

Second observation: Even though we, the local organizations, are the International Council—that is to say, we are the only voting members of this governing body—the International Council Committee is not really a committee of the Council, of the field, but rather a committee selected, convened, facilitated, and directed by the international organization, and one that is serving, in effect, at the pleasure of the international president and chairman. If we had a senate, we could establish a comparable senate committee really representative of the field—selected, convened and presided over by the field—with meetings convened and agendas addressed by dialogue and debate rather than force-fed by focus groups and facilitated by commissions.

This brings me to my third observation. Our international organization's governance proposal is designed to make sure that this never happens again. By this I mean a local organization proposal, like the Erie Proposal, getting on the agenda of the International Council Meeting without the approval of the international organization and its proxy, the

International Council Committee. If we had a senate, any local organization could get an item on the agenda of the International Senate Meeting without it being vetted by the international organization.

My fourth and final general observation is really an amplification of the first, and it has to do with something I've heard from Association executives all around the country. It is the perception that, if you vote against the international organization, you'll jeopardize future funding from them. I cannot imagine, having had the pleasure of working for and with our international president, Eileen Boyer, for the better part of three decades, any circumstances under which she would countenance that kind of quid pro quo. But because that perception persists, our governance is ethically compromised. Again, if we had a senate, we could have an open and honest dialogue about turning over these funding decisions to a disinterested third party. With only our current governing body, the International Council, this is a critical ethical issue that will never see the light of day.

Now I'd like to turn to the letter that I sent to the field to reaffirm a couple of points I made in defense of the Erie or what we prefer to call the Pennsylvania Proposal.

On page eleven of the meeting notice, The Erie Proposal was described as proposing "the establishment of an International Senate as the governing entity of the Movement." What we actually proposed in the letter that appeared on page twelve of the notice was the International Senate as an additional governing structure, not the governing structure of the Movement. It was not a proposed change, then, to a specific entity—in this case the International Council—of our constitutional structure, but rather, by adding an entirely new entity, a senate, it was a change to the constitutional structure as a whole. By characterizing both governance proposals as changes to the International Council and formatting them as one agenda item instead of two, the obvious misimpression was created—by a kind of political prestidigitation—that the two proposals were mutually exclusive; that a yes vote for one necessitated a no vote for the other. The truth of the matter is that the Erie Proposal was very carefully crafted so that you could in fact vote affirmatively for both proposals. I suppose one can conceivably look with admiration on political action so like that of the master Machiavelli when undemocratic dissembling is made to look benignly democratic.

I'd like to turn now to a couple of passages from a book by Morris Berman called *The Twilight of American Culture*, which I think has important moral and political implications for us as an organization and for other social and educational institutions.

Kent Carroll, cofounder of the New York publishing firm Carroll & Graf, has noted that publishing is now little more than brand marketing. It is no longer in the tradition of great American writers like Emerson and Whitman, not, in short, about the good life, but is instead driven by mass market sales of writers like John Grisham and Stephen King.

In 1981, according to journalist and media expert Ben Bagdikian, twenty corporations controlled over half the magazines published in the United States. By 1988 the number dropped to three. By 2005 most of the business in American newspapers, film, TV, books and journals were controlled by twenty-three corporations. As one literary agent put it, selling books is no different than selling popcorn (Berman).

We see the results everywhere. Campus book stores have become toy stores. Deans and college presidents model themselves on corporate CEOs and they use the odd doublespeak of corporate management with phrases like maximizing leverage or, as we have recently seen from our own international organization, Leveraging For Impact. As of the publication of Berman's book in 2006, most book publishing was in the hands of six corporations, most of them foreign (Berman).

Finally, Berman also noted that of the hundred largest economies, fifty-one were corporations rather than countries, and from urban affairs expert Dennis Judd he noted that "life within some sort of corporation is what the future will be increasingly about" (Berman).

If you love books, as I do, this is a troubling trend. But more troubling still is that this trend is happening to all of our social and educational institutions. It's happening to higher education. It's happening to public education, as illustrated by the heavy-handed propagandistic film *Waiting For Superman*, which our international organization not very wisely chose to endorse, and it's happening to us.

To illustrate how this is so, I'd like to read the last part of my letter that I sent to the field:

> As the political philosopher Michael Sandel has observed, when market forces define the structure and actions of our social institutions, as they most certainly have come to define us, then the democratic norms that once characterized an institution like ours become so degraded that they cease to exist in any substantive form.
>
> The ultimate irony, then, of our current approach to governance is that while our international organization touts civic engagement and citizenship development as a vision statement for the Movement, we have sat by while Whitehall has presided over the devaluation of the civic nature of our governance, essentially ending the

open public square we once had in the International Council, replacing it with a civic disengagement characterized by practices like proxies, electronic voting and governance by chat room.

We, the local Association organizations, were once the equivalent of citizens in a democracy, and because of that the legitimacy of our governance rested with us. Now we're treated as mere customers of a narrowly conceived business enterprise. But our relationship is not in any constitutional sense tied to purchasing any product or service. It is instead tied to a civic responsibility to govern. Not only are we not customers of this institution, we are actually the international organization's employers.

We don't then have to have our role in governance diminished to that of a shareholder in a big corporation. We can once again become stakeholders in a federation by voting for the International Senate and reestablishing a public square and a civic engagement commensurate with our vision as an institution.

The stark reality is that the kind of governance now offered to us does not privilege voice; it silences it. And it does not privilege real civic engagement; it effectively ends it.

So welcome to the branded, leveraged, systematized, standardized, quantified Youth Association International. And while you're at it, please pass the popcorn.

After the meeting adjourned, Eileen Boyer came up to me with a look both dour and aggrieved. She said in her iciest tone, "You made us out to be beasts," and turned and walked away. It reminded me of the fatalistic refrain in Vonnegut's fiction, the "so it goes" of life and death, of friendships damaged and of democratic institutions degraded down to corporate derivatives.

There is no metric for this, Mary Margaret. One simply cannot measure the depth of a friendship or the soul of an institution. As that wise old Stoic Seneca once said to the measurers of his time, "You geometers can calculate the areas of circles, can reduce any given shape to a square, can state the distances separating stars. Nothing's outside your scope when it comes to measurement. Well, if you're such an expert, measure a man's soul."

But no matter how one calculates it, Mary Margaret, what has been lost can never be regained. It is indeed hard to hold onto the good things in life, so please give my love and affection to that sometimes cantankerous old soul of a husband of yours.

Love you,
Michael

Hello.
Michael?
Yes.
It's Julia Scherer. I'm calling from the McSweeney's. I have, unfortunately, bad news.
Something's happened to Patrick.
No, Patrick's not doing very well, but it's not about him. It's about Patrick's and Mary Margaret's daughter Marlena. She was killed in an automobile accident this afternoon.
No, please, no.
She got in a fender-bender, got out of her car, and knowing her, probably to see if the person in the other car was okay, and a guy in a pick-up truck came barreling through on the berm of the road and hit Marlena and killed her instantly.

That Old Ghost Grief

More light!
~Goethe

22 October 2011
5 in the a.m.
in a well-lighted room
Dear Patrick and Mary Margaret:

Joan Didion, in a beautiful book about the death of her husband called *The Year of*

Magical Thinking, remarked that she has never been able to understand things until she writes about them. I share that malady, forever writing, jotting, scribbling. So, I write, seeking understanding and, in this case, solace.

My first point of reference is the death of my father twenty-three years ago. He spent his last days in a hospital bed, mostly unconscious and uncommunicative. I was at his bedside when his last breath rose out of him with a great sigh and disappeared. I picked up the phone next to his bed and called my brother. Not a single word came out of me, but somehow my brother knew who it was and what had happened and he arrived at the hospital shortly thereafter. After Julia called to tell me what happened to Marlena, I picked up the phone and called my daughter Diane, but once again there were no words for what was so senseless. I was stunned to tears, saddened by that old ghost grief.

A more immediate point of reference to this inexplicable tragedy is the death of my mother four years ago. I had not eulogized my father, so I was determined that my mother would have a more personal send-off. She was a tough old bird, the eighth of eleven children who died with dignity from cancer without so much as a single shot of morphine. I wanted, and I think she got, the best damn eulogies a mother and a grandmother could get, with eloquent and heart-rending eulogies from two granddaughters, Diane and Ellie. But the nights didn't go down so gently for me, and for a long time I had to sleep with a bright light on. I tried to give this regression a literary gloss. I am, after all, somewhat of a literary type, and therefore deal in gloss. Hadn't the great Goethe's last words been, "More light!?" Ah, I had become my mother's child again.

Although I had only briefly been in Marlena's company, I knew a lot about her from our conversations about our children over the years. What I knew about her was confirmed by the wonderful eulogies that were given after the mass and by your daughter Dorrie's comment that her sister had always been a bug in search of a windshield. As I see Marlena, she was, and remains, in the world of winds, a gale. She ruffled everyone's feathers while warming their hearts. She was big-hearted, kind, and loose-ended. She was what Shakespeare had in mind when he had Hamlet refer to humanity as a piece of work, for the Bard's words that followed, "in action how like an angel... the beauty of the world" seem to fit Marlena perfectly.

Know that I think about you guys every day. Once again, my light is on. Intuitively, I will know, as will you, when to turn it off.

With the heaviest of hearts and much love and affection...

Michael

Epilogue

The Fall

We are not going to defeat or overthrow
or even abandon the corporate structure,
in spite of its failures. This is a system
that continually grows stronger
while the society it controls grows weaker.
~John Ralston Saul

In the year that followed our failed attempt to reestablish democratic governance, my old friend and former boss, Eileen Boyer, a teacher and humanist early in her career and a committed corporatist at the end, finally retired after two failed succession plans and close to two decades as president of the international organization.

Eileen had begun her career as a social studies teacher in upstate New York, but by her mid-twenties she went to work for a national youth organization in New York City, and before she turned thirty she was hired as a program specialist for the Youth Association International, where she rose over the next thirty years to department head, to regional vice president, to senior vice president and finally to international president.

In the nearly three decades that I've known her, I don't ever recall a conversation about her undergraduate days at one of the SUNY schools. She was not in general very revealing about her life, but whatever education she did receive it did not seem to form a foundation for a life of the mind. She simply didn't read much of anything, as far as I could tell, other than the New York Times and an occasional novel. And she only read the Times, as she once explained to me, for what relevance it might have for her work at Whitehall. There was never any evidence of a broader curiosity or an interest in ideas in themselves. However dogged and detailed she was about her work, and she was legendary in the agency for her hard work, her analytical ability and her fastidiousness about the smallest detail, her world was made smaller by her lack of learning from books and her incuriosity about things not related to her work. Only in that narrowly prescribed world could one characterize innovation as the result of consistency, efficiency, accountability, measurability, systemization and standardization. Her legacy then was not as an innovator but as a fundraiser. She inherited an agency with a modest endowment of a few million dollars and left it with one totaling two hundred million, a pretty extraordinary accomplishment in less than two decades.

Despite a ceremonial reception at the international conference in honor of Eileen's retirement, it was, with the introduction of her successor the next day, an unceremonious departure, unceremonious because she was not so much gone as she was quickly forgotten. I didn't personally encounter Eileen until later in the conference when she stopped to say hello to me and my wife while we were having lunch in one of the hotel restaurants. After some small talk, Eileen bent over and whispered to me in a tone seeking confirmation, "Friends forever?" I whispered back, in spite of the fight we had just fought over the governance of the institution, "Of course." I saw in her last look, in her goodbye, a melancholic mood, and as she turned and walked alone down the open hallway that bordered the restaurant, she appeared to me, in her black pumps and black business suit, a forlorn, forgotten figure. I have not seen or talked to her since, but I think of her, now no longer my mentor but certainly my friend, often. Even though as she rose in power and in stature and ultimately fell into a narrowly prescribed world of corporate expedience, she remains for me what she wanted the kids we served to become, a good and gracious human being. And as I think about her and the life she led and the lives we all lead, I am reminded of the psalm that says, "As for man, his days are like the grass, he flourishes like the flower of the field; the wind blows over it and it is gone, and its place remembers it no more." And so she is, so we are all, like the grass.

Not her successor, though. Not John Moore. If his days, his persona, were like the grass, it would be grass made weedlessly verdant by regular applications of chemical fertilizers. At the opening session of the international conference in which Moore was introduced as the new president and CEO of the international organization, he presented himself in such sharp contrast to his predecessor that one was left with the impression that he was by indirection offering up a personal and professional critique of Eileen Boyer. Eileen, in all her years as CEO, was never comfortable on stage or center stage. She always stood behind a podium, a model of formality and reserve, and read her carefully crafted speeches from a teleprompter. Moore, a bespectacled, boyish-looking man of fifty, a buttoned-down but gregarious Midwesterner, stepped onto the center of the ballroom stage smiling and waving as if it were a place wholly familiar to him. And there he stood, in total contrast to Eileen, a wireless microphone placed under his blond head and beaming face, and talked for forty-five minutes from cue cards held by staff in the front row. To make the contrast more vivid, he brought onto to the stage more cute and cuddly Midwesterners, his spouse and children. Anyone in that ballroom—and there were more than three thousand that day—who had attended previous international conferences would have immediately noticed how different he was from Eileen, a reserved, dignified, divorced woman whose only son was never introduced in such a public way.

So standing center stage like some therapeutic pop psychology guru sharing his homespun wisdom, bookended by his wife and children, Moore had the two visual props he needed to distinguish himself from Eileen. Pretty clever public positioning, I thought: All American family guy versus the single, loner divorcee; and open and accessible to all of us local executives (Moore did in fact serve as a local Association executive for a decade) versus the reserved, remote international executive who never worked a day in one of the local organizations.

But there was more than just the visual set-up to John Moore's shtick. Family was also a major theme of his remarks. Over and over, like a literary motif or a song-like chorus, he told us that we in the Youth Association International were like a family now instead of the divorced couple we once were.

And then there was the granddaddy of them all: local, local, local. Whereas Eileen's perch, her perspective, her fundamental approach to just about everything after years of corporatization was top down, international to local, our new CEO, our dad daddy daddio, was going to make everything bottom-up with his new mantra, "local, local, local." As soon as he said this, and he said it early and often, I sensed then as a few others did, but only a very few, that we had entered the modern, Orwellian world of salesmanship, where words like "local" no longer meant local but rather the opposite, international. What we were witnessing was the rise of the salesman to a position of power, the salesman as CEO. This, it seems to me, is the final phase of corporatization: putting people in charge who have no real knowledge, deep or otherwise, of what a particular institution represents, but whatever it does represent philosophically and intellectually, the leader as salesman can at least superficially schmooze it to other corporatists; to, in our case, donors and funders. And if I had had any doubts about the Orwellian sophistication of this master manipulator, I no longer entertained them once I witnessed his handling of what was to become the last International Council Meeting in the hundred-year history of the Association. The meeting was held on the morning of the last full day of the international conference, which prompted me to write this letter to John Moore about a month after the conference:

Dear John:

Having had a chance to reflect on the recent international conference in San Francisco and the International Council Meeting in particular, I've decided to make a few observations about what I saw happen there.

As I sat in the ballroom in San Francisco and watched this year's International Council Meeting unfold, I was reminded of an International Council Meeting I attended thirty-five years ago. The meeting was held in a ballroom not unlike the one in San Francisco, a smaller venue, though, with fewer delegates, but the whole center section of the room was cordoned off with a small opening through which credentialed delegates passed, presenting their credentials as they passed through.

The gallery for observers, which spread out around the perimeter of the room, is where I sat that day observing my first International Council Meeting, a meeting which lasted most of the morning. What I saw that day thirty-five years ago, in the open dialogue and discussion and debate that unfolded, was a congress, an exercise in democratic governance that most if not all of our colleagues in the ballroom in San Francisco have neither seen nor experienced. But this is the kind of institutional memory that should never be lost and forgotten, and certainly not, as it has been in at least a decade, openly repudiated.

It would be difficult to characterize the kind of governance our colleagues have actually experienced in recent years. We have had governance by focus group, governance by commission group, and this year, a new low, governance by survey instrument. We were even told, as we sat supinely at our tables, that we didn't have to discuss anything under consideration; all we had to do was fill out the forms.

Then we had to listen to your International Council Committee representative—and it is by any definition your committee, not ours, since you appoint them, convene them, and wine and dine them—casually, condescendingly and unapologetically inform us that his committee would be vetting any agenda ideas coming from the locals. A policy of this kind has never been approved by the International Council, not to mention being appallingly and inherently anti-democratic. It censors not only what measures and ideas can be voted upon but also what topics we are permitted to talk about in the only international forum we have, the International Council.

But the *coup de grace* of the San Francisco meeting occurred when your board chairman suddenly reappeared on stage as the meeting was breaking up and the delegates were walking out of the ballroom—I'm using the term "delegate" loosely, since nobody, including the presiding board chair, had any idea who the delegates were or what organizations they represented—to ask if anyone had anything to say. Even if someone had something to say, to whom were they supposed to say it after the meeting had already broken up?

John, the form that any institution's governance takes depends on where legitimacy rests. When legitimacy rested with us, as it still does constitutionally if not operationally, as it did thirty-five years ago, we had an open and engaged form of governance characterized by democratic norms. Now that legitimacy rests with you and the international organization and your proxy, the international council committee, democratic norms have disappeared entirely, replaced by a corporate expedience averse to open discussion and debate.

How that happened and why it happened ought to be of keen interest to us, but it isn't. Instead this situation is met with widespread incuriosity and indifference, which makes it easy for you and the international organization to ignore it. Yet these kinds of questions go to the heart of who and what we once were and who and what we ought to be again, that is if we are to take ourselves seriously as an important social institution in a democratic society.

The reasons this decline occurred not only to us but to other social and educational institutions are undoubtedly complex, but let me suggest a simple starting point. We simply forgot where we came from, and remembering the democratic tradition we once enjoyed suggests to me that it would be wise to change the trajectory we are on in at least two important ways:

First, begin recruiting more people to our field who have a broader educational background in the humanities instead of narrow business specialists for leadership positions at the local, regional, national and international level. We need leaders who can do more than read a balance sheet and raise money. We need people who have a depth of knowledge about child development and a breadth of knowledge of and appreciation for western democratic traditions. We need people, then, as the archeologist and polymath Ian Morris has observed, who can see the big picture. "Those who stay within the boundaries of their own disciplines," Morris wrote, "will never see the big picture."

Second, disband the International Council Committee and start conducting, however inconvenient and messy it might be, a separate International Council Meeting with credentialed delegates, a democratic agenda open to the field and, for the first time in many years, a truly open national conversation.

Perhaps not many of our colleagues in the field would participate in this democratic process at first, but in time, with leadership and encouragement from you and your board, they just might come to appreciate and value the democratic spirit this institution once embodied.

My Best,
Michael Palermo

When I sent the letter to John Moore, I did so with modest expectations. I thought I would at least get a gracious if perfunctory answer from the schmoozy salesman-in-chief, something on the order of "thanks for sharing your insights on the governance process," or perhaps something like, "your longtime dedication and concern for our movement are laudable and greatly appreciated." This was, after all, the kind of thing that he was particularly adept at, gracefully and affably disarming you. John had, for example, seen me sitting in the hotel lobby during the San Francisco conference but took a moment anyway to sit down and ask me how I was doing. He did this even though he had heard me speak at previous International Council Meetings and was fully aware of the adversarial position I had taken with the international organization over the governance issue. John Moore always was, even with me, a model of cordiality, and so it came as a complete surprise to me that I never received an answer to my letter. I considered the possibility that he never received it, but when months later they conducted the next International Council Meeting on-line, thus ignoring everything I had suggested to him, I took his answer to be, to hell with Palermo and his democratic norms.

So now what? I thought about appealing to the people, in this case all the executive directors (though most now have the elevated corporate title of CEO) of that utopian entity Moore referred to as local, local, local. This could be accomplished by simply sending the locals my letter to Moore with the disclosure that he never extended me the courtesy to answer it. Instead he conducted the next International Council Meeting completely on-line. But to what end would I appeal to the people? I was, and remain, a contradiction: a populist without popular support, a leader of a lost cause. What could I expect to accomplish from an institution now led by business executives who have neither the knowledge nor the will to see beyond the narrow confines of their discipline: business. We've all been corporatized, deputized, standardized. We are incapable of seeing Ian Morris's big picture, a view of the world that could see not just how to do things like raise money and balance bottom lines but why we should do things as a social institution operating in the oldest existing democracy. With more generalists, more humanists, leading at all levels—locally, regionally, internationally—we could counter the crude scientism of the corporate world that dehumanizes children down to data points.

But countering is not the same as succeeding, and as the philosopher Karl Popper aptly pointed out, the equivalent of the democratic fairy tale is that rational argument can persuade people of good will to carry out in concert a plan of action, which, in this case of the Youth Association International, would be the reestablishment of democratic norms to a once democratically-driven, nonprofit institution. But if changing one institution is a limited but still unrealistic aspiration, changing the entire nonprofit world is a task only a tyrant could tame. Desiring neither the power of a tyrant nor having the moral or intellectual authority of a sage to bring fairly tales to life, I content myself with the power of the pen, with the McSweeneyian idea that to have never been a contrarian for a noble cause is to have had neither nobility nor integrity, and with T. S. Elliot's view that "our defeat and dismay may be the preface to our successor's victory." So, to my successors, I offer, as a summing up, these ideas not as moral imperatives but rather in the more quixotic spirit of why not.

Why not, for instance, reclaim charity's original meaning which could then be the basis of redefining what a charitable institution can and ought to be. Why not define charity as a compassionate act freely given without conditions or qualifications and without expectation of receiving anything in return on behalf of people with compelling human needs. This would redefine charity as an act based upon real human needs not institutional aspirations. This would have the salutary effect of driving charitable giving to the most vulnerable in our society, to the poor, the sick, the disabled, the abused, the neglected, the homeless, and the hungry, and coupled with the caveat that charity return to its original meaning as an act of compassion freely given without expectation of anything in return, charity would once again have the moral stature it long ago enjoyed. Today, unfortunately, we have conflated patronage, in which a donor's support is given in exchange for something—name recognition, a quantifiable outcome, an award—with true charity which is freely given. Patronage should never have the moral stature of charity nor should it ever be the basis for charitable tax deductions. Even more egregious is the practice of conflating charity with the sale of products like Pepsi, where the charity garnering the most votes on-line receives a "charitable" donation from the Pepsi Fresh marketing campaign, a practice which leads to the dual diminishment of charity and democracy.

Redefining charity as a selfless act instead of

one characterized by a quid pro quo would have the effect of reestablishing nonprofits as social institutions defined by who they serve rather than corporations defined by the business practices they employ. We would no longer need the corporation as a template for all of our social institutions. Why not try, as mightily as we can, to reestablish the noble idea that nonprofits ought to have intrinsic value, that they ought to have democratic norms supported by constitutions whose general principles diffuse power rather than concentrate it along corporate lines, thus ensuring that these constitutions never become compliance documents driven by dozens of standardized prescriptions? And why not once again recognize that the values of efficiency, accountability and measurability, which the corporate world has foisted upon the nonprofit world, have led inevitably to conformity not curiosity, to standardization not innovation?

We live in a Gilded Age far more ubiquitous than the one that came of age in the aftermath of the Civil War. While the former Gilded Age was one of monopolistic excess, the modern corporate age, enamored as it is with money, marketing and metrics, extended its reach with a kind of totalitarian excess into every aspect of our social and educational institutions. The missions and democratic norms of our institutions are now largely superfluous. All that really matters are the business bromides:

strategic plans, marketing plans, succession plans, outcomes, standards. One doesn't have to be a cynic to conclude that America is not a country; it is a franchise, a corporation, one that produces workers and career professionals, not citizens, not good and gracious human beings. The fall from what we once were, from what we might have been, is a centuries old decline, deliberative at first, but in recent decades a steep, relentless decline, much like the trajectory of my mentor, Patrick McSweeney, who is falling faster now along life's path of aging and illness, with the rest of his and our descent to come, death, and in time, oblivion. All a dead letter.

Life is a tender thing and easy to disturb.
~Montaigne

Long after the death of their daughter, too long apparently, I finally managed to break loose from the gravity of daily life—from family and friends, from work and reading and reflecting on things—to board a flight to Philadelphia to see the McSweeneys, to see Patrick, of course, and now, more than ever, Mary Margaret. As I flew from one corner of our beloved Pennsylvania to the opposite corner, Mary Margaret's reminders, her forewarnings of Patrick's current condition, made me wonder if this might be the last time

I see him, last in that the next time I see him he may no longer be him in any substantive sense. Mary Margaret reminded me that this is a disease in which the disappearance of the self is not a gradual descent that loved ones can readily assimilate, but rather more like falling off one horizon after another until what you once were disappears completely. It is a series of steep descents into the most heart-breaking and naked bewilderment. Mary Margaret told me that as long as I kept my conversation with him in the past, he could understand what I was saying and be largely, though not entirely, coherent himself. She also told me that as the day wears on he becomes less coherent. And finally she said the most disturbing thing of all was that Patrick still knew who she was and still knew who I was, which made me realize how tender, how tenuous his life now was as he approached what may very well be his last horizon.

On the way there I somehow set aside the roar of the plane's engine and the bump and sway of its small fuselage to summon up a memory of Patrick as he first presented himself to me more than thirty years ago, holding court in a hotel bar, a scotch in one hand and a cigar in the other, his suit slightly rumpled, his tie food-stained, his white shirt displaying cigar holes from fallen ash, and the distinctive sound of his voice, deep and mellifluous, and the incandescence of his conversation, equally deep, inventive, sometimes labyrinthian, that transformed the not-so-subtle shabbiness of his appearance into a persona refined, elegant, even courtly. He was, in that younger version of himself, both in appearance and in substance, a man in full.

I arrived in Philadelphia mid morning and by noon Mary Margaret had taken us to a place somewhere in the suburbs where Patrick and I had a leisurely lunch and spent an afternoon together, talking, remembering, drinking. We had lunch outside under the cover of a pavilion. It was a sunny, breezy, beautiful day. I kept the conversation, as Mary Margaret had advised, to the old days, as it were, when I worked at international headquarters in New York and Patrick served, and one would have to say led, two of my international committees. We talked about the vanities and political misdemeanors of the international presidents of the past, including our friend Eileen Boyer, whom we agreed was not, like the others, vain, calculating, insufferable. She was, by contrast, tough, dogged, ethical, smart, but in the end, either out of naivete or insufficient intellectual curiosity, a corporate apologist. There were long silences, too, while we ate and just sat together alternately warmed by the sun and cooled by the spring breeze. After one of these silences Patrick started to talk, not to me but to himself, like some Shakespearean character overhearing himself, lost in soliloquy, about a boy he had encountered in his career who had overcome great odds to become a successful businessman in the community. The boy's story, told with great care, was so precise and eloquent it could have been put down in writing as a polished, published short story. I later learned, when I told Mary Margaret about it, that there was no boy by that name, but rather he was the archetypal kid that Patrick and I and others like us had encountered over the course of our careers. He was Everykid to literature's, to life's, Everyman.

After lunch we moved to the bar at the other end of the pavilion where we spent most of the rest of the afternoon sitting silently next to each other, mindful only of the scent of cigars, the straight taste of bourbon for me and scotch for Patrick, and the cool, bright breeze of a sun-shaded spring. It seemed as though nothing more needed to be said. We were together, in our element, ever mindful that life, however tender, was, in its simplest moments, immeasurably good. But there was something more for Patrick to say. There was the matter of his daughter Marlena's death, whose name he seemed to whisper to himself as he turned to look at me misty-eyed and hollow-faced. He talked about Marlena in a way that a parent talks about his favorite child. And Marlena was, like Patrick, a contrarian at odds with life's conventions. But when Patrick's attention turned to the man whose recklessness caused the death of a daughter dear to him, his jaw jutted out, his nose flared, his eyes were ablaze with an intensity I'd never seen before. It was clear he had no confidence that the justice system would conduce to anything remotely resembling justice. Nothing, short of killing this man or having him killed, could console him. The thought that this was life's last chapter for the man I met when he was in the fullness of life, when his intellect was at its summit, when his children were young, when the future was promising, when life was good, only to have it all end with the death of his youngest, most cherished child and with the utter loss of who he once was, made me deeply, inconsolably sad, so much so that I could no longer look into those heartsick eyes of his, and so I stepped down from my stool and leaned into Patrick and gave him a long, hard hug. As I got back onto my stool, we both turned our attention to our cigars, to our drinks, to sitting silently together again, until a little while later Patrick poked at the silence for the last time, saying to me as if it were coming from his former self, as he had said to me many times before, "We're gonna win, Palermo. We're gonna win."

Bibliography

Berman, Morris. The Reenchantment of the World. Ithaca: Cornell University Press, 1981.

______. The Twilight of American Culture. New York: W.W. Norton & Company, 2000.

Bloom, Allan. Shakespeare on Love and Friendship. Chicago: University of Chicago Press, 1993.

Collins, Jim. Good to Great and the Social Sectors. New York: HarperBusiness, 2005.

Didion, Joan. The Year of Magical Thinking. New York: Knopf, 2005.

Eliot, T.S. The Letters of T.S. Eliot: Volume 4: 1928-1929. Edited by Valerie Eliot and John Haffenden. New Haven: Yale University Press, 2013.

Epstein, Joseph. In a Cardboard Belt: Essays Personal, Literary, and Savage. New York: Houghton Mifflin Company, 2007.

Gaddis, John Lewis. The Landscape of History: How Historians Map the Past. Oxford: Oxford University Press, 2004.

Galbraith, John Kenneth. The Affluent Society. New York: Houghton Mifflin Company, 1958.

Gross, Robert A. "Giving in America: From Charity to Philanthropy." In Charity, Philanthropy, and Civility in American History. Cambridge: Friedman and McGarvie, 2002.

______. Hall, Peter D. "The Welfare State and the Careers of Public and Private Institutions Since 1945."

Hedges, Chris. The Death of the Liberal Class. New York: Nation Books, 2010.

Hemingway, Ernest. Selected Letters 1917-1961. Edited

by Carlos Baker. New York: Charles Scribner's Sons, 1981.

Hirsch, E.D., Jr. Cultural Literacy: What Every American Needs to Know. New York: Houghton Mifflin Company, 1988.

Hughes, Robert. Nothing If Not Critical: Selected Essays on Art and Artists. New York: Penguin Books, 1992.

Keating, P.J., ed. Matthew Arnold Selected Prose. New York: Penguin, 1970.

Kuhn, Thomas S. The Structure of Scientific Revolutions. Chicago: University of Chicago Press, 1962.

Lucretius. On the Nature of Things. Translated by Martin Ferguson Smith. Indianapolis: Hackett Publishing Company, 2001.

Marcuse, Herbert. One Dimensional Man. Boston: Beacon Press Books, 1964.

Messina, Albert P. The Nonprofit Leader as Liberal Thinker: Politics, Ethics, and Strategy Reconsidered. Erie: Philanthropy House Press, 2011.

Mills, C. Wright. The Sociological Imagination. Oxford: Oxford University Press, 2000.

Montaigne. The Complete Essays. Translated by Donald M. Frame. Stanford: Stanford University Press, 1965.

Morris, Ian. Why The West Rules For Now: The Patterns of History, and What They Reveal About The Future. New York: Farrar, Straus and Giroux, 2010.

Murray, Charles. Real Education. New York: Crown Forum, 2008.

Nozick, Robert. The Examined Life. New York: Simon & Schuster, 1989.

Pallotta, Dan. Uncharitable. Hanover: Tufts University Press, 2008.

Popper, Karl. Popper Selections. Edited by David Miller. Princeton: Princeton University Press, 1985.

Ravitch, Diane. The Death and Life of the Great American School System: How Testing and Choice are Undermining Education. New York: Basic Books, 2010.

Rossiter, Clinton, ed. The Federalist Papers. New York: New American Library, 2003.

Ryan, Alan. On Politics: A History of Political Thought from Herodotus to the Present. New York: Norton, 2012.

Sandel, Michael J. Democracy's Discontent: America in Search of a Public Philosophy. Cambridge: Harvard University Press, 1996.

______. What Money Can't Buy: The Moral Limits of Markets. New York: Farrar, Straus, and Giroux, 2012.

Saul, John Ralston. The Unconscious Civilization. New York: Simon & Schuster, 1995.

Seneca. Letters From A Stoic. London: Penguin Books Ltd, 1969.

Tarnas, Richard. The Passion of the Western Mind. New York: Ballantine, 1991.

Tocqueville, Alexis de. Democracy in America. New York: Bantam, 2000.

Tough, Paul. Whatever It Takes. New York: Houghton Mifflin Harcourt, 2009.

Updike, John. Self-Consciousness. New York: Ballantine, 1989.

Williams, John. Augustus. New York: Vintage Books, 1972.